PARENTING BEFORE & AFTER WORK

PARENTING
BEFORE &
AFTER WORK

John & Carol Dettoni

VICTOR BOOKS®

A DIVISION OF SCRIPTURE PRESS PUBLICATIONS INC.
USA CANADA ENGLAND

Copyediting: Barbara Williams
Cover Design: Scott Rattray
Cover Photo: Tony Stone Worldwide

Library of Congress Cataloging-in-Publication Data

Dettoni, John.
    Parenting before & after work / by John & Carol Dettoni.
    p.   cm.
    Includes bibliographical references
    ISBN 0-89693-957-X
    1. Parenting—United States. 2. Dual-career families—United States. 3.
Parenting—Religious aspects—Christianity.
    I. Dettoni, Carol. II. Title. III. Title: Parenting before and after work.
    HQ755.8.D48   1992
    649'.1—dc20   91-46342

1 2 3 4 5 6 7 8 9 10 Printing/Year 96 95 94 93 92

Contents

Dedication

To Elizabeth Ann (Beth Ann) and David Benjamin, two beautiful and special people. Your strength of character, dedication to live for Christ, and your joy for living bring us joy. You've been master teachers about life and love. Through it all — the joy, tears, grief, despair, hope, challenges, disappointments, and fun — you've supported and helped, encouraged and challenged, always ready to live each new experience.

God immeasurably gifted and blessed us by letting us be your parents — to Him be thanks and glory.

Introduction

*"You are wonderful parents. I am so
thankful for you and Dad."*

Those beautiful words, repeated several times recently by our
twenty-five-year-old son, David, moved and touched me. They
were even more beautiful because the past few years rank among
the most stressful, sometimes out-of-control days of our lives,
ones filled with pressures, crises, uncertainty, misunderstanding,
heartache, and discouragement.

I think I sighed deeply and replied, "How can you possibly say
that after all the difficult times we've faced?"

David reassuringly answered my question as we discussed our
recent past. Our family of four has learned how to face the
difficult times together because of our love for and commitment
to each other. We have experienced John's close encounter with
death when he suffered a heart attack, and then supported him
on his road to recovery. Soon after, my father—the kids' dearly
loved grandfather—lived with us for the nine months before he

died a difficult death from cancer. And it has been necessary for both of our young adults to refill the empty nest while they attend seminary.

Through it all, we have forthrightly encouraged and supported each other, often just when we desperately needed affirmation and love. The lines of communication have been kept clear and open throughout the years. We have learned how to apologize, to hug each other spontaneously, and appreciate each other's tears. We have been vulnerable and faced our weaknesses and strengths head on. And most importantly, we've learned how to stop in the middle of difficulties, pray together, and ask each other's and our Heavenly Father's forgiveness.

We're far from being a perfect family. To the contrary, many times in recent years I have wanted simply to give up and run away from life! Particularly during those years when my two-minute, early-morning shower was the only time during the day I had to myself—to be alone and regroup for the stresses of a high-pressured job, the ever-constant shopping, cooking, lunch-making, washing, and chauffeuring. Add to that my church responsibilities, in addition to wife and mother roles. There just was not enough time!

Our children are young adults now—no longer children—and our lifelong parenting roles have shifted. Writing this book has helped us to look back and consider God's graciousness. Somehow we made it through their most difficult impressionable years, in spite of our horrendous schedules and the frenetic activity that accompanied us as dual-career parents. Temptations of drugs, alcohol, sex, materialism, and selfish pursuits were addressed and handled, some easily and others with great difficulty and hard times. On-again, off-again communication has now become stable, solid, and enjoyable. The values we strove to exemplify, both personally and as a family, have become assimilated in life's decision-making processes and lifestyle for both of our children. We are able to enjoy God's working out of His plans in our offsprings' lives. What an awesome experience to see our own, whom we dedicated to the Lord, in turn trust God for their lives with unswerving determination!

How did this happen? Why are we so blessed? I don't know

how many times I've asked God that question. It's probably due to a number of things—our open and sometimes-too-honest communication, loosening of the apron strings early as each child developed, and the earning of trust for each other, gaining understanding in each new situation that we faced. Respect for each child's individuality and trying to understand each person's needs rank high on the list of our conscious parenting decisions. Probably most important was listening to the child, to all of the big and little happenings and life stories that needed telling, particularly by our very verbal daughter! We shared in our children's dreams and thoughts as life unfolded with all of its mystery and challenge. We trusted them to make good decisions, and tried to understand the bad ones without being judgmental. We juggled our own schedules to be a part of their life events—demonstrating to them they were very special. One of us was always available to listen, hug, cry, and encourage—this was absolutely critical.

Where can the pressured and busy parent find time to live this way and get everything else done? Well, some things just *never* do get done. One has to come to a place of peace in accepting this fact. Personal letter-writing was abandoned for a period of time. Friends that would otherwise have been tops on the "communication" list took a place near the bottom. Sometimes this was misunderstood, and relationships suffered as a result.

Personal enrichment activities had to go—the things that I used to do "just for fun" had to be in conjunction with the kids' school activities, a lunch hour, or caught in-between times. Handwork, piano, painting, sewing, and reading for pleasure (even the newspaper comics!) became very low priority during these busy years. The gardening, which had to be done during the in-between moments, became my creative outlet.

Our personal social life slowed down considerably, with the exception of those times that were spent with parents of our kids' friends and classmates. Social life became band events—picnics with other parents while we watched our kids perform. Watching David at football, basketball, volleyball, and baseball games and practices became family outings, times to make friends and socialize, as did Beth Ann's many drama events. Occasional church social functions replaced personal entertaining.

Hospitality for out-of-town guests and formal entertaining of other adults became almost nonexistent. Instead, our little house became a place for the kids' friends to hang out. The formal dinner party our daughter gave for her friends was one of only a handful of entertaining endeavors during my full-time employment.

Family trips were visits to relatives in other parts of the country, or occasional weekends to the mountains or beach, with our kids bringing their friends along with them. As a working parent I was limited to brief vacation slots, which required working extra hours to attain. This meant I had to work some nights and weekends to accumulate time to take a vacation.

One year I decided to buy season tickets to the Los Angeles Philharmonic Symphony, something that John and I could enjoy together. Because of his travel and teaching assignments, and because of my deadlines, we were unable to use more than one-half of one concert. I gave that idea up as a lost cause!

John and I are committed to either professional or lay ministry within our local church. During those very busy dual-career days, we continued with this commitment. We both felt that our kids needed to be a part of our involvement by sharing alongside us. In retrospect, I think we made the correct decisions, even though life would certainly have been a lot simpler without such demanding activities.

So what have we learned? Parenting is love unbounded and unfettered. Parenting means sacrifice. Parenting is constantly making decisions. Parenting is one day at a time. Parenting is being transparent. Parenting can be all-consuming. Parenting is lifelong. Parenting is sorrow and joy, but a lifetime full of rewards. Parenting is commitment to your children, spouse, and self.

As you read this book, our prayer is that you can relate your experiences to the underlying principles that are addressed. This is not primarily a "how to" book but a "self-evaluation and application" guide. We've gathered research, looked at trends, and interviewed numerous single and working parents. Maybe your understanding of *who* and *where* you are in the parenting process can be better identified as a result of reading this book. And as you look at your own situation, you'll be able to find help and hope for this most important, God-given opportunity: *to be a parent.*

Carol M. Dettoni

Part One.
An Overview

One.
A Portrait of
Working Parents

Six A.M. The alarm clock shatters the sometimes fitful night's sleep. Mom was up half the night typing a paper for our teen-aged daughter (she must learn to type as soon as she can!). Struggling out of bed, Mom takes a two-minute shower, fumbles into the clothes chosen last night from the semi-organized clos-et, and she's ready for the day! Dad is shaving, showering, dress-ing, and packing for a two-day business trip.

There are four lunches to be made, the dogs to be fed, and our daughter wants to know if her outfit "goes together." (It doesn't matter what your answer is, because she will wear what she wants to, anyway, but she needs that reassuring, "Yes, it looks good!") Our son has forgotten to wash his band gloves, and he needs new knee pads for volleyball—today!

Sounding familiar? On an average morning at our house you would have seen this: everyone manages to gobble down something for breakfast—usually a bowl of dry cereal and fruit or instant oatmeal. All papers, homework assignments, bug collections, drama paraphernalia, sports equipment, and band music and uniform are gathered in piles and book bags by the front door, to grab as each person exits hastily.

Carol has a briefcase full of editing that she worked on last night, a salad to take for the potluck lunch at the office, and some information that she researched at home for a special project. John is off to Seattle today for a long weekend. (He leaves his carry-on garment bag always ready with essentials, so he just has to find some clean clothes!) He puts his itinerary under the magnet on the refrigerator, grabs his cardboard box of books, papers he's been grading, charts to return to his students, and he's ready to take off for the office.

Six-fifty and counting—the dogs are fed, the answering machine is turned on, today's outgoing mail is put into the mailbox. And John, David, and Carol are off to drop David at school for 7 A.M. band practice. Next stop—Carol meets her carpool at the freeway on-ramp. Beth Ann is left to close up the house and catch her ride to school.

It's a typical morning—no time for all four of us to sit down together and eat, and even with careful planning the night before, something is always left that becomes an "emergency." Frazzled and already tired, the working parents' day begins.

Getting to work is actually a relief, at least for a few minutes, until the busy office gets piled up with activity and decisions to be made. Carol will work through her afternoon coffee break; she has to chauffeur Beth Ann and her friends home from school today after their drama practice, so must leave work ten minutes early. (Fortunately Carol's employers are flexible and understanding.) John eats lunch at his desk while working. (He sometimes finds himself doing five things at once!) He has many details to take care of, including students and office staff to talk with, before his 3 P.M. flight out of Los Angeles International Airport.

Carol calls David's geometry teacher today at 10:10 A.M. on the dot during teacher break to find out how to help David with his homework. There's no way either parent can get to the school for a face-to-face teacher-parent conference, since work is a forty-five-minute drive away.

After work Carol drives to the high school, loads up five giggly girls, and makes the rounds to their homes. Then back to the school to get David after his basketball practice; a stop for hamburgers, and they're on their way home. Suddenly David remembers he needs a special notebook for class tomorrow, so out they go again. While they're out, they'll stop for a few groceries, and so it goes....

Nighttime—and clothes are waiting to be washed. (Each person is on their own with laundry.) The washer and dryer never seem to stop. There are phone calls to answer, the breakfast dishes to clean, homework to do, a committee meeting at church, choir practice for Beth Ann, church youth groups to attend, and always for Mom and Dad, a project that has been brought home from work, due tomorrow.

This scenario fits most working parents—grocery shopping on the run, housecleaning and gardening on the weekends or at odd hours, carpooling, school activities, clothes to be bought on lunch hours and work breaks—fifteen minutes here and there! And it all comes down to prioritizing the use of time, being a loving spouse, nurturing children, handling fatigue, keeping up with housework, and managing childcare. The inner yearning of the working parent is peace. And there's never time for it!

MAKING TIME FOR THE FAMILY

Remember Wally and Beaver, and Mr. and Mrs. Cleaver, those models of family life in another era? Like the typical '50s family, Carol was brought up in a time when women didn't have to work. When a girl married, her husband—no matter what his occupation—took on the responsibility of feeding, clothing, housing, and providing for his wife and family. The wife accepted life, "for richer or for poorer."

Today, only 10 percent of the homes in America fit the traditional "breadwinner" model, where the father goes off to work and the mother stays home to care for the children.[1]

When it was necessary for Carol to go to work full time, her mind-set was not that of forging a career, but of helping out the family financially. She thought it would probably be a temporary thing.

John came from another perspective — he was put in day care as a small child and his mother worked all through his school years. About one-third of the married women with children in his middle class neighborhood worked. Because of his experience, John decided that his wife would not work.

So it was that when Carol went to work, there was less of a value shift for John than for her. John already knew the positives and negatives for both the child and parents from personal experience. His mother worked because they needed the income and they wanted the extras that dual incomes brought, such as education for their only child.

Here we are at our mid-life, looking back at our experiences. How have our dual careers affected our family? How can our past experiences affect our young adult children as they face the ever greater stresses and opportunities of work, careers, and parenting that are ahead for them in the twenty-first century?

As society's expectations, economic pressures, and family structures have changed, so have many lifestyles, including ours. One traumatic event in our family was a result of job stress and of being stretched too many ways. John suffered a full cardiac arrest and a myocardial infarction at the age of fifty-one. It is by the grace of God that he is a positive statistic, one of a very, very small percentage that live through such an event without side effects and neurological and/or major heart damage. Did the sixty-plus-hour weeks, extra teaching loads to make ends meet, and frequent travels for his job add stress? Undoubtedly. His drive for excellence, combined with an aggressive Type A personality, made him doubly motivated to excel and a prime candidate for a heart attack, even though his weight was good and he had been exercising. We did not realize the role stress played in his life.

WHY DO BOTH PARENTS WORK?

Financial Necessity

Financial necessity appears to be the most prevalent of the many reasons both husband and wife work. In the average situation, it is the mother who goes to work out of additional financial necessity. The need for two incomes is partly due to the economic distress created by the high inflation of the 1970s and the social shift that has subsequently occurred. During our first year of living in a small, modest Southern California house, our mortgage, utilities, and real estate taxes were paid from John's salary, and all of the other necessities came from Carol's—food, clothes, gasoline, car repairs, clothes, etc. Others testify to the same experience—one respondent (in a survey we conducted) stated it well when he said, "Two salaries are absolutely necessary to live." In some parts of the country, this is certainly the case.

According to a USA Today report, "Most women today work because they feel they need to in order to make ends meet. . . . On the average, American households believe that they need $8,000–11,000 more in annual income to live comfortably."[2] Comfortably does not mean extravagantly. It means for most families the ability to do the "extras" beyond the bare necessities. As one husband put it, "I think we do have a choice. We could live on one income with some adjustments in lifestyle." But the reality is that many couples and almost all single parents find that working parents' incomes are really more of a necessity than an extra bonus. With the changing values mentioned in the next section, dual working parents have become the norm rather than the exception.

Changing Values
Mothers always worked in the past, but they found fulfillment in raising their children and being a homemaker, or as they were then called, a housewife. These "traditional values," which some would call old-fashioned or outdated, are no longer perceived to be acceptable by many Christian women and men in today's society. Women and men have accepted the idea that women can "have it all"—a job or career, fulfillment outside the home, a husband and children in the home—and be a responsible nurturer in all that they do.

On the other hand, in today's society our "wants" have often become "needs." There has been such an insidious acceptance of a more affluent value system that many people don't even realize what has happened. Many women enter the work force with their husbands "not because of dire financial considerations, but because of what have become accepted as middle-class needs (family vacation, college education for kids, cost of private—often Christian—elementary and secondary schools)."[3] Parents have adopted this value system, where the husband needs the weekly golf game to make business contacts, the family must have a boat or RV for recreation, Dad wants his sons to be in every sport possible—beginning with T-ball at age five, and ballet lessons are a must for the daughters. All of these are good things, but often they become perceived necessities because of social pressures and lifestyle choices rather than because they are actually necessary for the development of the children.

Parents sometimes work then, not for the extras, but for those things that at least they and their peers think are necessary for a normal life. It is this acceptance of a social value that often drives both parents to work, one of them at least half time.

Personal Fulfillment

"Many mothers work outside of the home for personal fulfillment, the desire to have a role that allows them to use their competence—years in education, training, and experience—in a particular field," according to Ruth Tucker in *Christianity Today*.[4] It is our experience and observation that mothers who have worked, either part or full time, have continued to grow and expand their lives as a result of the stimulating workplace and interaction with people. There is also a stronger sense of self-worth, particularly if affirmation is received on the job.

It is interesting to note that mothers of younger children are more likely to be employed part time, and less likely in career-related positions.[5] A number of mothers in our survey stated that they did not work while their children were preschoolers, but once the children reached school age, they felt free to do so. Others said that as soon as the children were gone from the home "permanently" then both parents would work.

Many mothers would choose to continue to work, but in a

part-time capacity. They do not feel fulfilled just with household activities and look for other creative outlets and interests. Other mothers are happy to go to work once the children enter elementary school. But these mothers want a job that will enable them to be home at about the same time that their children arrive home from school. This usually means part-time employment that coincides with school hours.

A number of women choose to work because it gives them a sense of challenge, of doing a job well, of self-worth, and of contributing to both society and to their families. They feel affirmed because they work and this feeling is important to them. They have a lot to offer, and do not want to waste their gifts, talents, and education. One mother commented on both her husband's and her own professional employment: "We work out of financial need as well as fulfillment and a sense of call." That sense of vocation is often missing from most discussions on working parents.

So it is that many people work not only to make ends meet and to have the "extras" for living, but because they have been called by God to serve in a vocation. They are fulfilled in a way that can only come from employment; it is their calling from the Lord along with that of mother or father.

Educational Needs of Children
Even though times are changing, attending college is considered to be a necessity for middle- and upper middle-class young people—this was true in our family. With the rising costs of college and university education, that second income becomes essential. Even with grants, scholarships, and student loans, many families cannot afford to send their children to a public four-year university, let alone one of the private colleges. In many parts of the country this has become true for private grammar and high schools as well. The education decision is a tough one to make, involving sacrifices for both the children and the parents.

Opportunities and Activities
A second income helps support opportunities that include music lessons, athletic involvement, school trips, church trips, camps,

and retreats, etc. These opportunities, though sometimes seemingly frivolous, can make a big difference in how your child relates to his or her peers, and can be expanding and life-changing in very positive ways. It's important to keep up on the communication process with your children to see just what these needs are. On the other hand, it is easy for the parent, sometimes out of guilt and as a "payoff" for their working, to go overboard in funding activities and special opportunities for their children.

Savings and Financial Security
Family savings are often totally dependent on the second income. There seems to be a shift back to personal savings and investments, after years of rampant credit card spending. For many families the only way they can save is with that second income.

Conclusion
As you think through the reasons why you work, we hope you will be able to understand yourself and your family in clearer focus. We trust you will find ways to lighten your load, and experience new hope in your particular situation.

It's a Fact

* In 1985, full-time jobs were held by 70 percent of working mothers.[6]

* Nearly 40 percent of fathers and 80 percent of mothers in Orange and Los Angeles, California counties said they would quit their jobs if they could, to rear their children at home.[7]

Why Do You Work?

Each spouse should work on this separately. Then take fifteen minutes to discuss together. Pray together. (For the single parent: discuss this with a trusted friend.)

Below are reasons why most people work. Using the space provided or a blank sheet of paper, write your own explanations.

The Reason I Work Is For

● Fulfillment _____

● Financial necessity_____

● Supplement for spouse's income_____

● College/other educational opportunities for children

_____

● Savings, security for our family's future_____

● Keeping personal skills, knowledge sharp and current

_____

● Single parent with no choice _____

● Other _____

Are You Happy or Satisfied with Your Parenting and Work Situation?

If not, why not? What can you do to change the situation?

Discuss the following:

1. Is my job the best use of my time at this point in life?

2. Would more work be better for the family and for me (if you're working part time)?

3. Would less work be better for the family and for me? If so, should I change jobs?

4. Do I want a career change? A better job? If so, what steps do I need to take to achieve this? Is my spouse supportive of this desire? What will this mean for the family?

Two.
The State of the
Working Family

Think of the changes in the American family during the twentieth century! Men, the traditional primary workers, were joined in the work force by a significant number of women during World War II, and women's participation in the workplace has increased ever since. Both men and women work hard and with determination. We are all to be applauded for our industry and ambition—Americans have achieved a lifestyle virtually unequaled throughout the world. But with that achievement have come other challenges. This chapter provides a glimpse of emerging trends, figures, and new configurations for the working family, and of how some of these challenges are being met.

How many dual working couples are there? The answer to this question may be surprising, since stay-at-home parenting is being chosen more and more. This trend is being looked at with delight by some parents. But in fact, more couples and single parents are working, according to the Population Profile of the U.S. (1984–1985): "Fifty-six percent of families had two or more wage earners in 1984—26.2 million families—while there were 17.9 million single income families."[1]

It seems that the traditional family—with the husband as wage earner, the wife as homemaker, and two or more dependent children—will continue to decline, if the research is correct. This family "equals less that seven percent of all households, and this proportion will not increase in the 1990s."[2]

WOMEN AND MEN AT WORK

The number of women participating in the work force (including those single and without children) is expected to rise to more than 60 percent by the year 2000 (U.S. Dept. of Commerce). At that time, women will probably constitute 48 percent of the nation's work force.[3] Any way we look at it, more women are in the work force than ever before and more mothers are working now than in the past.

Most fathers work because they have always been taught and experienced that fathers work. It never occurred to them that they would *not* work. If the father, like the mother, has a sense of calling from the Lord to a particular employment, then even more so the father feels he must work.

An interesting finding in one study showed that fathers who were "more satisfied and involved in their own work spent less time with their children than did less work-satisfied fathers; but their interaction was rated as more sensitive and more supportive of children's autonomy and affiliation."[4] One father stated that he was very aware of his role as husband, parent, and provider; he sought to spend time with his family each week, taking them out to eat or to some sports activity or to a movie. He expressed a continual need to know how to express love for his children, working at this, in one sense, to make up for the lack of time he spent with them.

THE SINGLE PARENT

"Only twenty-seven percent of households conform to the traditional image of a family—a married couple with children," according to a recent analysis of the California census. And only two-thirds of California children live with both parents. Nearly 1 million live with neither parent. Twenty percent live with one parent (up from 18 percent in 1980). Of 7.1 million households, more than 1.1 million heads of the household are women without husbands.[5]

The number of single parents has increased astronomically in the last two decades. Divorce, out-of-wedlock parenting, and death of a spouse all contribute to single parenthood, with most situations resulting from divorced or unwed mothers. The majority of these single parents are mothers, though fathers are increasingly asking for the sole care of children after a divorce.

Single mothers generally struggle so much more than dual working couples. These mothers have to be mother and father and often sole financial provider. They have to work and care for their children and house. Often they alone are responsible for teaching their children from the very basics of walking and toilet training to Christian values and a wholesome outlook on life. They must satisfy their children's needs for love, security, acceptance, affirmation, appreciation, family rituals, and the teaching of values as well as find ways to meet their own needs. They usually have little or no worthwhile support from outside people or agencies, including the local church, and often lack an adequate personal social life.

Some single parents treat their children as their confidants, seeking an emotional outlet and support. Not having another adult in the household with whom to share life and the experiences of that day, they turn to their children and confide in them.[6] By developing such an emotional support relationship with their children, it is possible for parents to disrupt and significantly (if not permanently) change the parent-child relationship. The child becomes the parent to the parent, and the parent becomes the child to the child.

The single parent's life presents a challenge—it is lonely and full time, with little outside encouragement and aid. Single parenthood takes a major commitment of time, energy, and financial resources. Yet it is not just a brave commitment against all odds. It is usually a commitment that has been examined from most if not all angles and is still willingly and lovingly made.

THE CHANGING WORKPLACE

Stress in its many forms continues to be a potential problem in our society. Transitional stress describes the parent who, when at work, wants to be at home more, but when at home, feels he or she should be at work.[7] Transitional stress showed up in a recent AT&T study of people with children under eighteen. The study found that 73 percent of the men and 77 percent of the women deal with family issues while at work. Twenty-five percent of the men and 48 percent of the women spend "unproductive time at work because of childcare issues."[8]

One mother expressed the contrasts that are felt with transitional stress when she wrote: "Motherhood is work, and having been in the business world for ten years and a full-time mother for seven, I'd take the ease of an eight-hour day, a full lunch hour, coffee breaks and all the social occasions and adult conversation that go along with working outside the home. So, why have I chosen to stay at home? Because women can't 'have it all.' . . . Since no one can be two places at one time, something has to suffer. If you let your job suffer, you lose it. Therefore it is necessary not to let your job suffer. The ones who suffer are the children, the ones who can't fire you for being insufficient."[9]

Both mothers and fathers are beginning to feel the inevitable tug between their dual responsibilities of family and work. They are like two masters vying for wholehearted commitment. Most parents know in their hearts that family should come before work. But they also know in the hard cold reality of the working world that if work does not appear to come first, they will likely lose out in advancements, promotions, and other job-related "goodies" that go to the "company man or woman." Dr. Joyce Brothers reported that in a recent survey, 80 percent of men and 87 percent of women felt that family and children were the most important things in their lives, even beyond work, career, and leisure time. Nevertheless they were " . . . often anxious about whether they were giving short-shift to their jobs."[10]

Parents live in a double bind that they find difficult to untangle. They love their families and they need their jobs. What can, what should, what (ultimately) will they do? These next pages will look at some of these changes and solutions in the workplace.

High Commitment Model

In his article, "Is Your Company Asking Too Much?" Brian O'Reilly states that "in the corporation the 'be-the-best' ethic has been warped into a dictate more like 'You cannot work too hard or too long.' The new corporate style dubbed the 'high commitment' model has sprung up, suggesting ominously that your life should revolve around work and not much else. At many companies the kind of punishing hours once reserved for crises have become the standard drill."[11] A 1990 *Fortune* magazine poll found that 77 percent of Chief Executive Officers feel they will need to push their managers in order to keep up with the international market. The irony is that we are working harder to compete in the international marketplace, while Japanese workers, who have used this model to a high degree, are experiencing stress-related burnout, suicide, or death from exhaustion. Many companies in Japan are encouraging more family time, long vacations, and lessons on relaxation for their employees.

In a nutshell, the media are painting the picture that corporations are asking more and more of their employees, while at the same time employees are questioning whether or not they want to continue at the hectic pace expected of them.[12] On the other hand, *Fortune* quotes Robert Kelley, business professor at Carnegie Mellon University: "The best are leading the move away from overwork. People are saying that sixty-hour weeks mean something is wrong with the system or with the person."

You may feel some of these same tensions. It's a tug-of-war, and the inevitable results of unresolved stress need to be prevented.

Flexible Hours

Flexibility offers a way to work around some of the heavy parenting—time—work conflicts. "A lot of people want flexible hours, not shorter hours," according to Charles Rodgers, vice-president of Work/Family Directions, the Boston-based counseling and consulting company.[13] Many are already achieving this. For instance, nurses are working longer shifts for fewer days (often three days), in order to have those precious days off lumped together for involvement with their families. Having such a schedule with flexibility means the parent often feels more like working and comes to both the job and home with renewed energy and productivity. For many, flexible workdays or hours make a big difference in the quality of family life.

Teleparenting
Teleparenting is a term used for the "at work" parent who consistently parents from the job.

Teleparenting is not just having an occasional phone call at mid-afternoon to let the parents know that all is well at home. It is also repeated telephone calls to the workplace to ask questions, discuss problems, ask permission to go somewhere or do something, tattle on one's brother or sister, and for a whole host of other reasons. A wise parent perceives the child's need for security and reassurance, and finds balance in the number of calls and time taken away from the job, so as not to take advantage of an understanding employer.

Teleparenting is a lifeline for both parents and children who are at home unattended. Not all of the phone calls are really necessary, but are actually ways of establishing contact with the missing parent or parents—a way to say, "I need you and since you're not here, I'll call you so you can let me know that I'm important."

By 3:30 P.M. on many school days, the phone would ring in at least one parent's office. It would usually be our daughter calling to let us know about her day at school, the "exciting" events of the day, about the crazy things her friends had done, or about Mishi, our missing cat. She felt secure, knowing that she could call at any time and that we would not react by being bothered. In fact, we encouraged her to call. Our son used the phone as well, though his calls were usually not as long. He more often than not called in for advice or permission to do something. The phone contact was a very effective way to keep track of our children's activities and their "ups and downs" each day.

Teleparenting provides access to the parent, security, advice, and a listening ear. It gives structure that would otherwise be totally absent. A writer states, "Latchkey kids are actually just a subset of a generation of youth being raised by parents from work."[14] The good news is that parents are able to do this. For many decades, there was not as much access to the phone as today. Parenting, by phone or by notes from parents who are absent from the home even for a short time, is still parenting. And children of working parents gladly receive parenting whenever possible.

Coworkers are often aware of problems that others' children are facing and become a support group at work, giving advice and showing general interest. These friends become like an "extended family" even though they may not know the children. More than once coworkers have supported us through difficult parenting times with their prayers and understanding.

Working at Home

The at-home job is becoming more and more desirable to many people. According to the Barna Research Group, "In 1990, an estimated six million households have at least one head of the household using the home as a work base; by the year 2000 there will be an estimated twenty million."[15]

Four hundred parents who worked at home were surveyed in 1990 by Stein and Espindle. They found that the vast majority thought they could better balance family and career from the home workplace, and that their children liked the fact that they were working at home. Those same children said that the parents were better at parenting because they worked at home. Children were perceived by their parents to have a better understanding and appreciation of their parents' work. The downside is the fact that parents felt that time management and a sense of "being spread too thin" persisted in one-person, at-home businesses. Not enough personal and leisure time were still large problem areas.[16]

Some parents in our survey work at home, yet they still have live-in help to care for the children during the day and occasionally at night. In one dual-career family, the father is home most of the day and keeps an eye on the youngest child, who is also being cared for by the live-in person. In this case the wife is a professional with office appointments and regular hours away from the home each day.

So while working at home solves some problems of balancing career/job with family, it does not solve the number one problem of time. Time for parenting still requires attention and that attention means that career and job cannot be the focus of one's thinking and emotions; the family must be the number one concern.

Being an entrepreneur — having your own business and being your own boss — offers many positives, both for parents and children. Rather than delving into the pluses and minuses in this book, our personal experience shows that it is crucial to have a careful business plan, and an objective, realistic understanding of what is involved. Often, the entrepreneur, at least at first, spends an inordinate amount of start-up time. The discretionary time to spend with family is there, but it may take several years to realize the desired results of such a working option.

Job Sharing

Some younger professional couples are beginning to cut their hours by about half in order to share a job with each other. This is still an exception in the workplace — not very many couples hold the same kind of job. But for those who do, this setup enables them to share parenting and household responsibilities as well. More commonly, some people are sharing a job with a non-spouse, someone who also wants more hours to spend at home with their children. This trend is just emerging, however, and not everyone has the type of job which can accommodate sharing. For those who do and can afford to take a cut in pay, job-sharing is a positive option.

Other dual working parents have decided that each would work at their jobs between twenty to thirty hours per week. They have found employment where this half to one-third time is possible. Those who attempt to follow this approach need to be sure that they will have adequate benefits, especially health care coverage.

Paternal Leave and the Mommy Track

The paternal leave benefit is a hot topic in today's work world. Only recently have fathers begun to take advantage of time off when their children are born. The paternal leave is not widely available yet—fewer than 20 percent of big and medium size companies offer even unpaid time off. Even in corporations where the paternal leave has been instituted, those who take it are not always looked on by the employer with great favor. In fact, a father interviewed on "Nightline" said that when he took paternal leave at the birth of his son, he was encouraged to call it a "vacation." In his opinion the traditional view of senior management is that "any man who would take paternal leave can't really be that serious about his career."[17]

Mothers who take their maternal leave risk being shuffled to the "mommy track." Women on the "mommy track" readily admit to being career and family focused. They have decided that they will give up the fast-paced, hard-hitting, competitive, and time-consuming lifestyle of the business or professional world. Instead, they opt for flexible hours, reduced work commitments of time and tasks, and less-rapid advancement in their level of promotion. They see themselves first as nurturers of their children and then employed women. But they do not want to give up work altogether. They are, however, willing to forgo more salary and faster promotions in order to be mothers.

Many of these women will continue to work part time with the idea that within one to five years they will return to full-time work. By doing this they preserve their careers and their spot in the promotion ladder, though they will be more on a plateau than a ladder while they work part time or totally take time off from work. They will be able to maintain contact with their business or profession. Technically, they do not quit their jobs. They just take a slower track to advancement. Currently, there are many different ways for women to design their "mommy track" and just how this is done depends on the employer and the woman involved.

Another innovation in the workplace is on-site public schools and day-care centers. Companies provide the physical facilities and necessary equipment. The local board of education and state provide teachers and the curriculum. The first such company-funded school for employees' grade school children was established in Miami in 1987 by Bankers Insurance Group of Miami.[18] This idea, if it is successful, could be an answer for many families in the future.

THE POSITIVE PICTURE

Can good come out of the juggling of work and family? Yes, there are many positive outcomes, even though there are definite drawbacks, many of which have been explained. Being a child in a family in which the only parent or both parents work is not all bad. A study of children who grew up in dual working homes reports that families realize they have limited time and therefore choose activities for their families with great care. They realize that time is of the essence.[19]

This study also reported that the children interviewed, looking back on their earlier years, did not resent what they felt was their significant role in sharing responsibilities and household duties. In fact, the children were quite positive about their parents' dual-career lifestyle. They felt that their families had high strength, especially in their mutual concern, respect, and support. On the other hand, parents felt that the children had to become self-sufficient much earlier than was ideal.

Divorced working mothers and their children perceived that the children had more responsibilities and were less involved in outside activities than children from intact families, according to another study. However, the study showed that the actual time spent in outside activities by the children of divorced, working mothers is no different from children in intact families. And responsibilities such as taking care of the yard work are fewer for the children of working divorced mothers than their counterparts in intact families.[20]

All working mothers, in both intact and divorced families, reported that their children had fewer friends and were less involved with other children than the children of non-working mothers. It is difficult to know whether the reported differences are real or only perceived. At-home mothers have firsthand observation of what and with whom their children are involved while working mothers may not know the extent of their children's actual involvement with others. The reported difference may not be an actual difference but might be a matter of perception by the mothers.

Children often report a high esteem and respect for their dual working parents or single working parent. They see the sacrifices. They see tired parents and realize that some things are left undone because their parents work. Yet they recognize that the money is often needed for required things (or at least for perceived needs). In return, many children bestow an admiration and respect on their working parents.

Many parents work, as chapter 1 points out, because they need the money. Ask them what is good about working and they will tell you, "I can pay my bills, make ends meet, and be able to live. We have a roof over our heads, clothes on our backs, and can afford occasionally or more often some of life's luxuries. I work to get these and they are all positives."

Some parents are less monetarily oriented and more philosophical about the positive results of their working. One husband stated that he and his wife share the household duties equally. From his perspective, his children see a marriage that has both parents on an equal basis, not one superior to the other, and this is good.

Parents' working provides the opportunity for many children to achieve accomplishments in areas where they would not otherwise excel—how to care for oneself, fix simple foods, help prepare meals, take care of one's own clothes. They learn that each person has the ability to help and a contribution to make. One father reported that his four-year-old sets the dinner table and clears his own dishes, as well as picks up his clothes.

Dual incomes provide higher living standards and more financial stability. More expensive family vacations can be taken. Educational enhancement is achievable—the children can go to private schools rather than to what are sometimes perceived by parents and children as less-than-satisfactory public schools. One parent said that their children could engage in school sports because both parents worked and had additional income. To use his words, "Sports even cost more money now."

Parents often save for their children's college expenses with money from the second paycheck. An annual college bill of $16,000 in 1992 is expected to rise to $50,000 and up in fifteen years, when today's five-year-old enters college. Many middle-class parents see the need to save for their children's college education, knowing that the middle class has lost out on much student financial aid for college expenses.

One of the greatest positives of the working parents is that children see their parents pulling as a team when both work. This is true not only because both bring in an income, but even more so when both shoulder the parenting and household duties. Children realize that fathers see their mothers as women of value in their own right. Children see that many mothers have fulfillment in their work outside the home. When both parents work, often a new sense of the mother's importance to the family is present, and this without diminishing the father's importance.

Children also see the tricky balancing act that parents live with in order to provide basics and often extras for their children. They realize—or will someday—that their parents love them enough to provide for their financial and material well being.

It's a Fact

* "By 1986 ten million families, or one in every six, were financially supported by women."[21]

* In 1988 "seventy-two percent of women aged 25–54 (both with and without children) were in the labor force. Sixty-eight percent of mothers with school-age children and adolescents were in the work force."[22]

* Some experts predict that by the year 1995, "eighty percent" of women between twenty-five and forty-four years old will be in the work force, the majority of them mothers and some of them part time."[23]

* "In 1976 thirty-one percent of women returned to work within a year after their baby's birth; in 1985 the figure was eighty-five percent."[24]

* "The work week increased from 40.6 hours in 1973 to 46.6 hours in 1987; professionals worked fifty-two hours; small business owners and corporate executives, fifty-seven hours.[25]

* The Family Research Council[26] found that parents spend 40 percent less time with their children than they did twenty-five years ago. In the mid-1960s the average parent spent thirty hours a week with their child; now they spend seventeen hours per week.[27]

Where do you fit into the working family picture?

Answer these questions below. If you are a dual working parent, share your answers with your spouse after you have both answered individually. (Some of the questions will not apply to the single parent.)

1. Are you a dual working family? Yes _____ No _____

2. If yes to number 1, how many hours per week do you and your spouse each work?
I work _____ hours per week.
My spouse works _____ hours per week.

3. How do you feel about the decision that you should be a working family?

4. What tensions do you sense between working and parenting? Briefly describe these tensions.

5. Do you feel like you are in the "high commitment model" of work as described in this chapter? If so, or if you think that you easily could be soon, what steps can you take to get out or to avoid getting into this mode?

What *will* you do within the next week to avoid this "high commitment model"?

6. There are some alternatives available to the working parent to make juggling work and parenting a bit easier. Which are open to you?

Flexible hours
Job sharing

"Mommy track"
Working at home
Paternal leave
Maternal leave
Other _____

7. What steps will you take to explore the alternatives? List these steps. What will you need to know in order to accomplish an alternative? How will you go about finding this information?

8. What are the positives about your being a working parent? Consider the positives for the following:

Your children
Your own self
Your spouse
Your family life
Your house, garden, etc.
Anyone or anything else

9. What are the negatives about your being a working parent? Consider the negatives for the following:

Your children
Your own self
Your spouse
Your family life
Your house, garden, etc.
Anyone or anything else

10. If you or your spouse were to stop working or even to significantly reduce the number of hours you work each week, what would happen to the positives and negatives that you listed? Could you, your spouse, and your children live adequately with the change? What adjustments would have to be made? Are these adjustments likely to happen?

Three.
Problems Parents Face

Most frustrations of the working or the single parent seem to focus on one word—time. There is simply not enough of it to do all of the things that are demanded of working parents. Closely allied with lack of time is the fatigue factor. That comes when the busy, stretched parent is pushed for time. The two go together, and seem to be the top problems facing working and single parents.

An informal survey of busy working parents, conducted by the writers of this book, found the following to be true: The respondents had little time for their spouse or children, and even less time alone to spend on themselves.

"People in growing numbers are finding themselves stretching to be both productive at work and happy in their family lives," says Fran Sussner Rodgers, President and Founder of Work/ Family Directions, a counseling and consulting firm in Boston.

"Remember the old game show 'Beat the Clock'? Just imagine playing 'Beat the Clock' every hour, every day, day after day. That's literally what the lives of many working families are like."[1] It's true—because of the many demands, and the *kinds* of demands, we just never can catch up with or stay on top of everything, even though we are organized, motivated, and most often, well-educated working adults.

It seems a strange conflict. At work—within the structure of the workplace—focused achievement and success is possible. But at home it's different. There are mundane chores and details of daily living to deal with, as well as the blending and communicating demanded by differing personalities within a household. Parents are tired and stressed; children need constant attention. Parents become *reactive* to life instead of being *proactive* and in control of time and many large and small details. And too often the spiritual dimension of life becomes slighted or nearly overlooked in the business of the "daily grind."

Many dual and single working parents have reprioritized their time and activities, determining what is important and cannot be left undone (for instance, the buying of food). They also must decide what can be left for another time, such as washing the car. And finally, they can add to the list of things to be done "eventually, when I get around to it." Not every working parent makes an actual list, but most have a "built-in automatic filing system" into which they put each thing that comes their way.

The following are some of the major stressors and problems that face working parents. By reading and identifying where you are as a working parent, it is hoped that problem areas can be identified and action taken now to avoid what for some could be tragic repercussions. These major areas are: housework, childcare, time for family, job conflicts, leisure and social time, time for oneself, handling of details, and spiritual life.

HANDLING HOUSEWORK

Many families "spend evenings and weekends trying to stay caught up with housework," according to a report cited by Ambrose and Mueller.[2] Over and over again, the people whom we surveyed said that housework and gardening suffered because both parents worked. The "deep down cleaning does not get done as much as it may need it" is a common statement from working parents. Parents tend to do what is absolutely necessary, such as the light cleaning, filing of bills and stacks of papers, mending, ironing, cleaning cabinets, minor household repairs, touch-up painting, and major gardening and landscaping changes. Standards of personal neatness for the household and yard often are unachievable. Fix-up work, cleaning the garage thoroughly, and major home improvements—all these are left for another day. One wife stated it well when she said that housework, "The giving of the extra touch that makes a house a home," suffered from both parents working.

In the authors' survey of parents, respondents reported that they spend some time on weekends and Sundays catching up with housework. Some try to clean in the evenings. But many said they just never get it all done. They are too tired, and they simply run out of time to do it all. The big stuff and really dirty and soiled things get cleaned. What is "not that bad" or what is not so easily noticed gets left until later—much later, if it ever gets done.

We were surprised when several parents told us that nothing or as little as possible is left undone when it comes to the household. These people either are so organized that they can do it all, or they have adjusted well to what they can and cannot do and they may not notice things that others might. When John was young, he knew a family with dual working parents whose house was in a constant state of disorganization, bordering on chaos. Yet neither parents nor children seemed to think disaster was just a hair's breadth away. For them, disorder was the way they ordered their lives. It is possible, then, for some parents to get everything done. It is also possible that they have developed an ability to prioritize. Like Mary and Martha in Luke 10:41-42, some parents choose "what is better" rather than being "worried and upset about many things."

Women still do 90 percent of the work around the house. They handle most of the shopping and almost all of the care of the children. Thank goodness this seems to be changing: we have found that many husbands are taking a larger share of parenting and housework responsibilities. This seems to be particularly true of younger couples, where they may have married later and have lived on their own for a while, so are already used to doing their own cleaning, cooking, and grocery shopping. Hopefully, the trend will catch on quickly!

Adequate Childcare

Above all else, most parents want what is best for their children, in all aspects of life. That is why the childcare situation is of critical importance and a struggle for working parents. Since childcare is a national problem, much discussion is ongoing concerning the situation — but it's not likely to change very quickly, particularly for low income families. "Only about twenty percent of childcare programs in the U.S. are of adequate quality," according to Eric Nelson, director of Child Education at Cal Tech-Jet Propulsion Laboratory Community in Irvine, California.[3] "One hindrance to childcare quality is the pay — childcare workers earn less on average than janitors, house cleaners and garbage collectors."[4]

Childcare is an expected concern for the working parent, and includes the administration of discipline as well as the quality of the care. One mother reported that she does not like the way her housekeeper/caregiver disciplines her young child, but she has to overlook that fact because a good housekeeper is hard to find.

Many parents have relatives or childcare givers with whom they are comfortable. These often come to their homes so that their children stay at home with live-in help. This is not to downplay the very real need for quality childcare throughout the country, but simply to state that it seems that most people who can manage it will resolve the dilemma through either a church family network, relatives, housekeeper, nanny, neighbors, or a combination of the above. We found in our research that "most parents are happiest when a relative, baby-sitter or housekeeper provides care in the child's home. . . . Parents whose children are cared for at home are frequently dissatisfied with its cost, but they are rarely happy with anything else."[5]

Increasingly, nannies are being employed to live in the home, care for the child or children, and do some basic housekeeping. Professional nanny agencies, listed in the Yellow Pages of the telephone book, place these women, and occasionally men. Sometimes married or single graduate students are employed as live-in baby-sitters and children's caregivers for late daytime hours and evenings when both parents are away.

What are parents saying about their situations? Parents whom we surveyed saw childcare as a major problem, especially for younger children. Parents stated that the childcare they used was not the way they would do it if they cared for their own children. One wise mother said that she gives various kinds of support to the childcare providers for her daughter. She also "adopted" teenage "sisters" who would come to her house to be with her daughter so that she would not be uprooted from her home environment.

The jury is still out on the long-term effects of being cared for in a childcare facility. For the most part, experts do not have adequate research available to make a determination—it will probably take a second generation of children of working parents before researchers are able to measure the actual effects. The potential for child abuse should not be overlooked. Many books are written on the subject and would be good to skim. Just keep in mind that you need to know your children and listen to them, even at the earliest ages. Trust your children. And find help if you suspect a problem.

Many parents are dissatisfied with their childcare situation, and may experience what *Fortune* magazine speaks of as the " 'vexing loss of productivity due to parents' worrying about who's minding their kids.' Working parents seem to be trying to assuage their guilt by cutting corners on the job."[6]

To address this concern, many companies are beginning to provide childcare for their work force. For instance, Ted Childs, Director of Affirmative Action and Work Force Diversification at IBM's U.S. headquarters in Purchase, New York, said "that the company (which has gone from thirteen percent female workers in 1965 to seventy percent in 1991) discovered 'it is in our enlightened self-interest' to pursue and develop packages that involve child and elder care."[7]

LACK OF TIME FOR THE FAMILY

One of the first things to be slighted by working parents is the quantity and, even worse, the quality of time spent with their children. This was reported over and over again. One mother said that because of her work schedule they would have to eat dinner late if the family was going to eat together. When mothers or fathers work on Saturdays and Sundays, the family seems to suffer even more. These two traditional "family days" are taken from the family with no days to substitute for those lost to weekend work.

Working parents—both mothers and fathers—feel they do not have enough time with their children. Care must be given, however, in interpreting this statement. There are sufficient suggestions in the research literature that show that when only one parent works, the children do not get "that much more" time than with dual working parents. It may be that working parents are more tired, feel guilty (and many admit this readily), and feel like they would like to or should spend more time with their children. Whether they would find the time if they did not work is another matter altogether.

There is no doubt that as we have reviewed the family literature, surveyed parents, and recalled our own dual-career family lifestyle that time is a major issue for parents. Many are sensitive to being parents and know that it takes time to be effective and wise. But there cannot be more hours in the day or week to provide this time. It must come from somewhere. One father said he just sleeps less hours per night in order to do more. Another said that there just were " . . . not enough hours in the day to do what I am required to do at work and home." Another mother said that she was torn between "how to make more time for myself to work on concerns regarding a promotion without taking time away from the family."

When time conflicts arise between job, family, and personal time, invariably personal time suffers first followed by family time. The last time demand that suffers is the job. Parents report that when they "teleparent," or receive calls from their children regularly at work, the amount of stress placed on the parents' time is increased. Often employers realize the importance of these phone conversations between an employee's children and the employee. It's no wonder that parents report feeling stress and fatigue from carrying the burden of the time needed to be effective parents and also effective in the workplace.

HOW PARENTS' WORKING AFFECTS CHILDREN

The development of a high sense of self-esteem in children takes time and encouragement. And according to *Fortune* magazine interviews with "educators, psychologists, drug experts, executives and troubled teens, that's the most important thing a parent can do for a child."[8] A parent must be aware of the child's development and needs. "Serious emotional problems usually start when children are in the sixth to eighth grade, and hit crisis proportions by the sophomore year of high school. . . . By junior year they're on track or in serious trouble," according to Sheila Ribordy, a clinical psychologist at DePaul University.[9] (As you read chapters 4–7 on child and adolescent development, keep in mind that the most critical issues in parenting occur during the early teenage years.) These problems require time, not money, from parents.

The way a parent relates to children and teenagers often means a total shift from relating in the workplace. "The attributes a manager must develop to succeed include perfectionism, impatience, and efficiency," says Andree Brooks, author of *Children of Fast Track Parents*. "Contrast those traits with what it takes to meet the needs of a growing child: tolerance, patience and acceptance of chaos."[10] No matter what your children's ages, it takes focused time and ability to truly enjoy the parenting experience. Otherwise the child will know that Mom and Dad are not really "there" with them, but instead are thinking about what they should be doing for their work or at home.

The time parents' spent with them seems to be important for kids as they look back on their lives. According to one troubled seventeen-year-old son of a high-ranking executive, "The best manipulation parents have is their attention. It is an extraordinary power that most of them neglect to use. Parents are very important to kids—more than they will ever let on."[11] One wonders what the simple use of more time spent with family could have meant in many situations.

Along with lack of attention and time devoted to children come some rather strong statements that echo the working parent's fears. Tom Collins, Executive Director of Fairview Deaconess Hospital (an adolescent and drug treatment center in Minneapolis, Minnesota) says: "Every move you make away from kids in pursuit of your own happiness and career increases their chance of getting into trouble. Lending kids out to babysitters and day care makes it a crap shoot."[12] Can Christian parents legitimately engage in a crap shoot with their own children? Can we allow ourselves to focus on material things to the detriment of our own spiritual lives and our children's development? It makes us think, does it not?

Research shows that somehow many families DO find the time for what they feel is important. (We took the time to be parents to and for our children—even when we did not feel we had any time to spare!) It seems that when it comes to time management in the home, "Working parents use various coping strategies, including reducing time in personal, leisure and community- activities, in order to be more available to their families."[13]

Though time is probably the biggest piece to fit into the working parents' puzzle, there seems to be enough time available to make it happen, if tapped properly. And that's the hard part, requiring thoughtful evaluation and action.

LEISURE TIME, SOCIAL LIFE

Social life is also affected by lack of time. In fact, respondents in our survey reported that they have very little social life, either with spouse, family, or friends. And if fatigue is a major problem with working parents, one can imagine how this affects interpersonal relationships within and outside of the family.

Many parents have been married long enough for three things to have happened. Number one, their children are now older elementary age or in their teenage years. Number two, the parents may have grown accustomed to each other and take each other for granted. They stopped doing things together when they were younger because they did not have the money and the children were too young, etc. Now that the children are older, they have not changed the old patterns. They are still in love with each other; they just do not go out much anymore. Number three, there is so much to be done at home, they are tired, and the kids need so much attention that the parents spend all their extra hours keeping up. They do not socialize, even with each other. More than one parent in our survey stated that quality time with the spouse is a major area that suffers, along with contact with friends.

One mother said she tries not to feel guilty about wanting time as a couple away from children and the pressures of work, home, and children. And one husband responded, "You have to push harder for good communication when there isn't as much time for it because there's more opportunity for misunderstanding." He pinpoints one major outcome of insufficient spousal time: ineffective or bad communication. Tired, stressed spouses do not make for fun and exciting companions.

Many parents try to schedule social time for themselves and their friends, but they are not always successful. One husband stated that he simply does not have a social life and has no close friends, only male acquaintances. Some parents limit their social time and have no independent social life outside their children's world. One plaintive statement came from a father who said: "Unless someone invites us to their house, we have no social life. We go out to eat periodically." His wife added that they often eat lunches together and that is the extent of their social life. In our experience it became normal to turn down invitations rather than accept them. After a while, people stopped inviting us because they knew we couldn't accept. This seems to be a common experience for many.

But even though time may not allow for extensive social life and leisurely pursuits, outside relationships are still important. Research shows that "families that report they have quality relationships with relatives and friends dealt best with the stresses of family life."[14] This should not come as a surprise, for after all, we are social beings and God intended for us to live in a community.

The extended family—grandparents, aunts, uncles, and cousins—have been vitally important to our nuclear family, particularly during times of great stress. But our extended family has been too far away to help with the everyday needs for support. A lot of working parents do not have family close by, either, or do not have a close relationship with their extended family, whether geographically near or distant. And this leaves a void that is hard to fill, but filling it is vital.

TIME FOR SELF

Working parents do not have enough time alone just for themselves. They are always either fixing or getting something ready, nurturing, or doing any of innumerable tasks. But seldom do any of these tasks include caring for oneself.

Because of insufficient time for oneself, parents reported feeling fatigued with an exclamation point after "fatigue!" Not only do they feel physically drained but also emotionally, psychologically, and spiritually drained. Each of these three areas of fatigue makes a vicious circle, each leading to the other with seemingly no way to stop the cycle.

Both mothers and fathers reported that they tried to take personal time when they needed it, but they did not report a high success rate. Their intentions were good; their practice was bad. One mother said she "scheduled it [personal time]. But I don't schedule rest and relaxation time; only errands, etc."

When parents take time for themselves, they usually do it at hours when the children's demands are near zero. This means very early in the morning or later in the evening or when children can be cared for by a baby-sitter. One mother wrote "I usually do not make time for myself," and then she drew a teary eye on the paper.

Perhaps that sums it up: we know we should take personal time, but we most often do not; we know we miss it and we know we will pay for it in the end. We just seem to hope that it will not catch up with us before we can make lifestyle adjustments. The trouble is, we do not know how long we have until this will happen. Then when physical or spiritual-psychological catastrophe hits, we make the adjustments. When ulcers, heart attacks under age sixty, psychological breakdowns, depression, unrelieved fatigue, repressed anger, unfathomable loneliness amidst busyness, and divorce hit us, we have to make time for ourselves or we will cease to be whole persons and even possibly die.

Exercise, eating properly, caring for oneself, and the whole family are so important, but often become low priorities. For many working people, coffee breaks become addictive—caffeine is the drink of choice or seeming necessity. The fact that so many people do not take care of themselves shows in the number of younger men who suffer cardiac problems. In our case, we thought we were doing the right things, but found out after John's heart attack that we were eating the wrong things for high cholesterol. So even in active, sports-minded, and health-conscious families, there needs to be the watchful eye on health, diet, and exercise. Each person must find a way to relax, unwind, get good sleep, and keep in shape—a walk through the mall at lunch or a five-minute snooze on a break—whatever it takes to be active and in shape. Face your stress head on, find out what is causing it, and see what can be done about it. Find someone to talk with, including a counselor who can help you sort through your personal needs.

FEELING GUILT

Working parents are probably some of the most guilt-ridden people around. They have guilt for not doing all they, their spouse, and children expect of them. Guilt for a less-than-perfectly clean and tidy house. Guilt for not having enough time to go to all of their children's school events. Guilt for not being able to work on a church committee, teach Sunday School, or be active in the P.T.A. Guilt for praying on the run and for sandwiching Bible reading in between making sandwiches and cleaning up the breakfast dishes. Lots of guilt for not being perfect parents according to standards and expectations.

If they take "self time" parents feel guilty. It seems like there is a little voice inside every good parent that says, "You should do more for your children, your job, your house. Sacrifice yourself. You can do it." And as one person said, "I feel guilty not being able to do it all." Unless parents can still that treacherous voice inside of themselves, they will drive themselves to feelings of guilt that aren't true but nevertheless are just as damaging to their whole personhood.

It's a Juggling Act

Parents report using weekends for just about every imaginable activity from getting their own hair cut to visits with relatives, friends, and one-on-one times between parent and child. One father takes one of his six children to breakfast each Saturday morning when he is in town. Because he travels he does not make it fifty-two times a year, but he gets in about forty to forty-two breakfasts. That gives each child about six or seven Saturday mornings, just with Dad! Not too bad for a busy executive father.

Many of the routine household necessities get done on demand, and Saturday seems the most frequent day to do these things. Probably in no other arena of family life is there more creativity shown than in the shopping for personal and family needs. Some parents squeeze out time for errands, others will pay a baby-sitter for a short period of time.

Parents complain that they just cannot seem to plan anything. Things just happen. One mother said, "I find time *only* when it becomes absolutely necessary, at which point something else suffers." Perhaps she spoke for a whole host of mothers and fathers!

Some parents find an effective defense mechanism for handling all that they feel they ought to do: they procrastinate. They feel that if something does not get done and the world has not stopped yet, then they are fairly safe in thinking that it was not necessary to do anyway. This works — as we all can testify — for a while, for some things. For others it's disaster!

There seems to be a growing willingness among some parents to "hire out help" to get the work done. Baby-sitters have been around for many years. But increasingly parents are hiring housecleaners and/or nannies. They shop by mail, even grocery shop by telephone. And service industries have sprung up to do all sorts of work for busy people.

FACING SPIRITUAL DROUGHT

Sundays have become more than a day for worship and spiritual input. They look like Saturdays for many people, Christian and not. Regardless of the fourth commandment to keep the Sabbath holy, working parents find that they have to do things on Sunday that their parents would never have thought permissible in a bygone era. These parents, if pushed to justify their action would appeal to Jesus' teachings on the Sabbath and its purposes (Luke 6:1-11; 13:14-17; and 14:1-6) in which strict keeping of the Sabbath was reinterpreted to be viewed from the needs of people and not just the keeping of the Law. Regardless of one's view on the Sabbath, the practice of many Christian working parents is to combine worship, household chores, shopping, and rest, sometimes all on Sunday.

The spiritual life of the parents and the family is often a casualty when the parents work. Seemingly higher-priority issues take so much time that we quite easily leave the family's daily spiritual nourishment for a more convenient time. That more "convenient" time never seems to arrive until Sunday morning when we bustle off to church. Family devotions or even a short time of prayer each morning often do not fit into the schedule of working parents and their children.

If you are like most working parents, you have found yourself described in many different ways and on most of the pages in this chapter. There is actually good news for all of us. First, we are not alone. There are millions of working parents who share these similar experiences and feelings. Second, we *can* do something to change our circumstances. We do not have to "go it alone" or be passive and/or reactive. As you think about the questions at the end of this chapter, reflect on them in both the light of this chapter and of your experiences. We pray you will find the Lord's help as you find ways to be even more effective in your complex roles of parent, spouse, and worker.

Think About It

Answer the following questions. If married, work individually, then share your answers with each other.

1. What gives you stress in your life? (tensions, pressures, anxieties, distresses, frustrations?) Briefly list as many as you can (or that you have time to list). Consider the following possible sources of stress: work, spouse, children (any one in particular?), social life (or lack thereof), finances, health/personal care, household duties.

2. What causes these stresses? Think not so much of the circumstances, but ask why do those circumstances produce stress for you.

3. To what degree do you feel that you have to be a "superperson"—a supermom or superdad? Where did you get this idea? Have you accepted it? Is it driving you or are you in control of it?

4. **For husbands only**—To what degree do you readily help your wife in what used to be called "women's work"? Mentally trade places with your wife. Would you want to do all that she is expected to do each day at home and work? How can you and the children help alleviate some of your wife's stress that comes from being mother, wife, and homemaker? (If you are already mutually sharing the load between spouses and children, you get a "gold star" for the rest of your life!)

5. If your children are in a childcare setting, either at home, at neighbors, or relatives, or in a professional day-care center, how often do you inspect that care? Do you look for sanitary conditions? Safe conditions? Overcrowded situations? Adequately

trained staff? Proper food preparation and handling, and good, nutritious food? Do the childcare workers understand child development and your Christian values? Do the caregivers help your child/children to grow and develop as whole people? Do they give them spiritual nurture as well as nurture in the other areas of growth and development? (Check chaps. 4–7 for more on development.)

6. What changes in your workplace can make your working and parenting easier? What would you and your supervisor/boss have to do to make these changes? How soon can you begin to implement those changes?

7. Consider your parenting time each workday. How many minutes each day do you *actively* parent your children? Do you feel that they receive enough of your attention for them to grow and develop normally in all aspects of their lives (physical, mental, social, emotional, moral, and spiritual)? Think of two or three things that you might do to help make more time for them. What plans do you have to make to get this additional time for wise and effective parenting?

8. When was the last time you went on a date with your spouse or, if a single parent, with a special friend? If it was not in the last two weeks (and we are being generous here!), what can you do to go out together in the next seven days? Do not think of an expensive restaurant. How about a starlit walk or a movie or a community concert? Keep it simple and inexpensive — that way you will be able to repeat this "date" without having to worry about costs.

9. When was the last time that you took time for yourself when you were not hurried or having guilt feelings? Why was it so long ago? What can you do to change this, and how soon?

10. Are there any other ways to juggle all the household chores? Can your children be involved in some of the more simple shopping? Consider taking a few hours in the next few weeks to teach older children how to help out more.

11. In what ways can you help make Sunday more of a day of rest than a day to "catch up" on all the loose ends from the last six days (or months!)? Realistically, what can you shift to another day or put off indefinitely so you can have a more relaxed, family oriented Sunday?

12. How well are you functioning as a good steward of what God has allowed you to earn as extra income? Does God receive what He should from your earnings?

It's a Fact

* "Ninety percent of wives and eighty-five percent of husbands today say women do all or most household chores"[15]

* Twenty-four million children under age fourteen had working parents in 1984. Of these children, 23 percent were in family day care, 6 percent were in childcare centers, 42 percent were cared for by relatives and other arrangements in their own homes, and 29 percent were under self-care.[16]

* In a poll of parents, 95 percent agreed with the idea that a good chat about school or other children's issues is important. But only 75 percent managed to talk with their kids about school and other children's issues. While 86 percent believe it is important to have regular family dinners, only 66 percent actually do. And while 65 percent felt it is important to attend church, only 48 percent said that they actually attended.[17]

* The characteristics of good emotional health in the home include: "strong marital coalitions in which fathers and mothers share a parental leadership, clear generational boundaries between parents and children; responsiveness and clarity in communication between family members, and the freedom to be open about feelings."[18]

Part Two.
Parenting with Understanding of
Your Child

Four.
Making the Most of
Your Time

Rapid change! More happens developmentally during childhood and adolescence—in the first twenty-two to twenty-five years—than in all the other years of life put together. Working parents need to understand these tremendous changes in order to work *with* them and not against them. God created us to develop from less to more mature, from less developed to more fully developed. Parents are the primary aids for their children in that developmental process. What parents do will either help or hinder their children's growth. In particular, parents will either aid the Holy Spirit in their children's spiritual development, or will hinder—or even worse, quench—the Holy Spirit. It's critical that busy working parents understand how a child grows. Knowing how to meet the challenges of each age can save precious time and headaches.

Understanding your children's developmental processes demands action: "Anyone, then, who knows the good he ought to do and doesn't do it, sins" (James 4:17). Parents who want to be wise and effective will understand and function according to the developmental stages of their children.

How Do Children Grow?

Children grow in predictable patterns but not in predictable time periods. This means that regardless of the child—assuming no pathology that would affect normal development—all children follow basic, predictable patterns of growth. They do *not* follow a standard timetable. Some children develop more rapidly and others more slowly, but each normal child will develop in accordance with his or her own internal timetable. Parents should not be concerned if their child's pace of development is slower than others of the same age.

The parents' responsibility is to help, to facilitate, to channel, and to instruct their children as they grow. Parents should not try to control or manipulate or, worse yet, speed up that process of development. All too often parents seek to find ways to make their children into little adults as quickly as possible. This is a common fault that compares to the home gardener who overwaters and overfertilizes his plants. The result of such anxiousness to get bigger and faster-growing plants is just the opposite: the plants either rot and die or have lots of green leaves and no fruit! Parents should not push for growth, but work with the growth process.

What Makes Children Grow and Develop?

Growth and development occur from within and are seen in externally observable things. For example, as children receive food, their physical bodies begin to grow and muscle development occurs. Parents watch their newborn infants change almost before their very eyes as the children begin to gain weight, to increase muscle strength, to focus their eyes on moving objects, and much more.

In one sense, child development occurs automatically. Yet while growth and development are natural, they do not happen in a vacuum. Development occurs as a result of interactions between people and their environment. Parents establish and maintain the environment for their children. And if parents do not give proper nutrition, children will not grow and develop physically. Parents are the nurturers of their children, they provide the environment and encouragement for growth.

Busy working parents need to be especially aware of these external influences. Parents, older and younger siblings, extended family members, friends, school, church, neighbors, toys, books, and the media—especially TV and films—provide the stimuli that engage children's developmental mechanisms and stimulate their growth and developmental processes.

From a child's earliest age, parents help this process to continue—people and events influence development, especially interaction with people and things in the child's environment.

Children grow when they receive stimuli which challenges the way they deal with and make sense out of the world around them. These challenges, whether physical, cognitive, moral, social, affective, or spiritual, are the stimuli needed to continue to develop. God has created within each of us a normal, innate ability to recognize these challenges and to seek to resolve them by either growing and developing or by ignoring them and, as a result, not changing. All children, assuming normal childhood, have the built-in capacity to develop.

What Can Busy Working Parents Do?

Parents need to continually provide enriched experiences with things, books, people, toys, ideas, and places and help their children experience these to the limits of their developmental capacity. This takes time and priority for busy parents. But they can provide input that stretches their children—not too much, but enough to cause some stimulation. Parents help and encourage their children to physically develop, to stand up and take a step or two. It would be foolish to expect a child to walk unaided at six or seven months, but it is quite reasonable to expect that child to walk while holding on to something or someone.

The process of learning to walk illustrates how parents, and others in the children's environment, help a child learn something new. The helpers provide stimuli that are in accordance with where the child is developmentally. What holds true for the physical area is true for all other areas of development. Children develop because they are ready to, and because they receive stimuli that cause them to recognize that they can develop. Without the outside stimuli, normal development will not occur.

Children enter into the world quite dependent on caregivers. As we've already said, the God-given process to grow and develop is already implanted. The caregivers, normally parents, need to recognize these processes and to understand how they work. They should know their roles as parents, the helpers and facilitators of development. (Parents should make outside caregivers aware of the growth process for their children.) Parents need to know that the goal of development is for their children to: "Become mature, attaining to the whole measure of the fullness of Christ. . . . In all things grow up into Him who is the Head, that is, Christ" (Eph. 4:13, 15). The goal is not for children to be like their parents! They are to be like Christ, the goal of development for both parents and children.

Turning Children to Christ

Children do not automatically turn to Christ. They need to be cultivated like a very expensive, rare, and precious plant, not "trained" like some sort of wild vine. They are not wild; they are just sinful like anyone else. Yet they have within them an "automatic homing device" that centers on God. Parents need to help their children focus on God, working with that inner sense of God that He created within each person when He created all of us in His image.

Children's earliest understanding comes from their five senses: taste, sight, hearing, touch, and smell. God created us to be able to experience new sensory data from the earliest moments of birth—recall the wail of the newborn infant who is whacked on the bottom to get his or her lungs working. Parents constantly provide new sensory experiences in the child's world. Many of these experiences can focus on the Lord. God is seen in Scripture as the nurturer, caregiver, sustainer, provider, encourager, teacher, and disciplinarian. Human parents, paralleling our Heavenly Father, need to fulfill these same roles in order to help their children grow and develop into the persons that God wants them to be.

WHAT CHILDREN THINK ABOUT THEIR PARENTS' WORKING

The very young infant, placed in childcare, probably has no idea of what is happening. Since the world of this child (from a few weeks old to even several months) is limited to that of the five senses, a parent's absence is not seriously noticed. It is not until the child begins to recognize and remember faces that permanence is attached to a parent's presence or absence. At this point, a child becomes affected in some way by the working parent. But it is difficult to predict just what that effect will be. Some children are secure and accepting of just about anyone and anything. Others, even in infancy, are more fearful and less secure. These children have a more difficult time adjusting to being apart from their parents. As one mother wrote in our survey, one of the major problems she has in working is her child's response to being left at childcare. Her daughter cries and apparently fears abandonment.

Parents, Infants, and Day Care

One way to help infants adjust to a day-care setting is to help the child get used to being around other people. Often a parent realizes what is about to occur and seeks to make up for a future lack of attention by spending all of his or her time with that infant. By the second or third month of life, the child is used to being the center of attention and to parents being at beck and call. When the child is placed in infant day care, the whole world completely changes. Out of many competing centers of attention, he or she is only one. This is a rude shock to a two- or three-month-old. The shock is unnecessary if parents are careful not to overcompensate and spend an inordinate amount of time catering to their child's whims before the child is placed in childcare.

Parents need to avoid the feelings of guilt that are often

associated with infant childcare. Perhaps parents suddenly realize that they really do not want to place their child in childcare
but it is necessary. If this is the case, then parents should recognize that they live in neither a perfect nor an ideal world. The
reality is that some parents have to work—single parents in
particular usually have no other choice. It is better to make the
best of a less-than-ideal situation.

Infants need to become accustomed to different people caring
for them. Remember that most parents do not have problems
leaving their infant children in a church nursery for one or two
hours. Most children can and will adjust to their infant care
environment if properly prepared. If there is a problem, it often
is not with the infant but with the parents who do not want to
relinquish the child.

Perhaps the more shocking event for parents of infants is to
find that their children readily go to a childcare worker, just as
they do to their own parents. Somehow parents think that their
children should not want to be left with childcare workers and
should return to their parents with eagerness and relief at the
end of the day. These parents fear that the love normally expected from child to parents is being channeled to the day-care
workers instead.

Some parents observe that their feelings are similar to those
of the firstborn child who fears that the newborn second baby
will absorb all the love that his or her parents showered on him
or her. The parents understand and know that love expands to
include all new offspring, and that they can love the first child
just as much as before. But when it comes to sharing their child,
particularly the first one, with a caregiver, they often balk. They
think, "How could my child seem to show an equal amount of
affection to a 'stranger-caregiver' as to me?" What the parents
do not realize is that their child is not replacing—nor has any
intention of replacing—parents with day-care workers. The
child recognizes a friend in the childcare worker and responds.

Childcare for the Preschool and Elementary-Age Child
Preschoolers and early elementary children may well respond
differently to childcare than infants do. As a five-year-old, John

recalls being taken to a day-care center. He dreaded that moment each day. Though he had friends at the center, he did *not* like the setting. He recalls eagerly anticipating his mother's arrival each afternoon to pick him up. And he can still remember the smell of her clothes as he climbed into the car to go home. That smell meant security, acceptance, and love to him. John understood that both of his parents needed to work. But he *did not* want to be in that day-care center.

Was John's experience the norm? It is difficult to generalize from one experience. But he recalls that none of his young friends in that same day-care center were very excited about both of their parents working and their having to be cared for by others. With his mind he understood it had to be; with his heart he was saddened.

Children Reflect on Their Working Parents

Research has discovered that often children have several responses to both of their parents working, depending on the children's ages. One young adult female reported that she really hated to have her mother working. When she was a child she wanted a mother who lavished all of her attention on her children. But now as an adult, she was glad her mother had worked, and she herself was now planning to work as a wife and mother. She added that working was an important part of the happiness of the dual-career parents' marriage.[1] Many children in a study of dual-career families stated that they intended to choose as their lifestyle a combination of marriage, work, and family.[2]

Older children, primarily ages sixteen to twenty-four, reflected on their family's dual-career lifestyle with positive responses. They saw that their parents provided role models for the world of work as well as models for nurture. The males especially recognized the equality of their mother with their father since both brought in incomes. This sense of equality spilled over into other social and work relationships with women. They became fully aware that women are not inferior and have significant roles to play in society as well as in the home.

These children also recognized that their family's lifestyle encouraged their own development of independence. They saw the financial benefits from two incomes and responded to the fact that at least their material and physical lifestyle was enhanced by their dual-career parents. And they noted that their families had strong commitments to each other, appreciated each other, showed mutual respect, concern, and support, held each other in high esteem, had positive communication patterns, and were able to resolve conflicts.[3]

The usual problems of dual working parents were apparent in the study by Patricia Knaub from which these facts are drawn. The children reported four major problem areas as they looked back on their childhood. *First* was the time element. Parents often had prior commitments and could not attend their children's school and extracurricular functions. *Second,* parents were often tired by the time they got home or on weekends, and thereby reduced the amount of time and energy available to give to their children. *Third,* the children insightfully recognized that their parents did not have enough time to spend alone with each other. The thing that makes for strong families—namely, their parents' relationship as husband and wife—suffered from lack of time. *Last,* the children saw that communication difficulties arose between children and parents. The study also discovered that a *fifth* response was present from a significant number. These children said that they did not see any problems associated with a dual-career family.[4]

What can we say then about children's perceptions of their parents' working? As older children look back on their earlier experiences, they can see the benefits of dual working parents. The pain and sadness of the past is viewed in a new light. And strangely, these children seem to agree that the experience was good for them. They even intend to repeat it with their own spouses and children.

Conclusion

The developmental processes are fascinating to watch but the working parent often does not have the time to stop and look. A helpless, newborn infant turns into an adult in twenty-one years. Wow! Parents have only a few of those years for primary input into their children's development. Understanding the developmental processes and our parental contributions to them is rather crucial and worth the time spent, as we shall see as we look at the next three chapters.

Think About It

Check Up on Your Understanding of Development
Answer the following questions based on the material in this chapter. Couples, answer individually and then share your responses with each other.

1. Do you tend to look at your children as developing in predictable patterns *and* within a fairly predictable time table? Do you find yourself looking at charts of children's growth and comparing your child or children to the "normal" child? If so, why do you?

2. Can you do very much to significantly speed up your child's development? Why or why not?

3. List three or more things that help make children grow and develop.

4. "Nurturing" is a very good word to describe parenting. What does it mean if you were to say, "I help to nurture my children"?

5. What specific things could you change in your child's or children's environment to encourage steady development? (Think of toys to use, books to be read, audio and video cassette recordings to listen to and watch, and other experiences.)

6. Assuming that your child or children are old enough to talk and to think a little for themselves, ask: What do they think is *good* about your working? What do they *not* like about your working? (You may want to tape this session.)

7. Ask your children what they are receiving because you are working.

8. Ask your child or children what they would miss if you were not working.

9. What do you make of your children's replies to questions 6 through 8? Write down in outline form what your children said and your interpretation of it. If you recorded their comments on tape, be sure to mark and place the tape in a safe place. In a year or two, ask them these same questions again and compare their replies.

Five.
Encouraging Your Child's Growth — on the Run

Parents are supposed to be helpers in the growth and developmental processes as their children progress from less to more mature. This chapter gives a brief look at two of the six areas of development: the *physical* and the *cognitive* or mental development.

Physical development is obvious because we all can see what is happening. The mental, though less observable than the physical, is nevertheless also easy to observe: a child begins to look at things, begins to examine toys in the cradle, recognizes faces, etc.

Parents may not identify all of these actions as part of cognitive or mental development, but psychologists do and so shall we. Look first at children's physical development beginning with infancy. We will seek to determine how busy parents might respond in those nonworking, parenting hours.

Physical Development

Young Preschoolers

Wigglers. Preschoolers are physically active. If God tells children to wiggle, but parents or others tell them to sit still, they will listen to God. And listen they do. Preschoolers are always active. They look for and need large muscle activities because their large muscles are developing. They cannot thread a needle or write their names, but they are wonderful at arranging and rearranging blocks, pots and pans, and anything else that they can get their hands on. Starting with their legs and arms, as soon as they can crawl or move themselves by scootching on the floor their whole bodies are constantly moving about.

Children do these actions for two basic reasons. The first is that their large muscles are developing—this is physical development. They are trying out new ways of relating to their environment. The second is that they are just plain curious about their environment. Children do not empty out a cupboard because they are naughty or sinful. They do so because the cupboard is there and it is full of things they want to explore.

"Hungry" Senses. Preschoolers have "hungry" senses. That is, they are actively looking for sensory experiences. When we look at a child, we should be reminded that we as human beings are made to be sensual creations. (We as parents also look for and enjoy new sensory experiences.) Children's lives should be filled with things that they can handle and touch, see, smell, taste, and hear. When parents return from work each evening, it would be well for them to set up a ritual in which they sit down with their preschool children and provide some parent-child sensory experiences. True, a good day-care center or baby-sitter will provide these types of experiences. But the time alone with one or both parents cannot be replaced with a "hired" parent. The way to continually help one's children to develop is to be in charge of their environment. One way to do this is to provide sensory experiences within a loving home environment.

Short Attention Span. Your preschooler does not plan out his or her responses. They see something and want it and then reach for it. They do not think, "The stove is hot so don't touch it." They see what they want and go for it with all the gusto that their little bodies can muster. This also means that their interest spans are very short. They are always on the lookout for new and changing stimuli.

Everything in their world seems to belong to them, and they want to see, touch, taste, smell, and hear it all. Thus they often go quickly from one thing to another. Parents may sit down to read through a ten-page "scratch and sniff" book and the child will start looking for something else after page 3. The parent may feel rejected or think that something must be wrong with his or her child's attention span. Wrong! The child is normal. It is the parent's response to the spontaneous and flexible child that is "wrong." Parents need to go with the flow of spontaneity and flexibility that characterizes children at this level.

Making Music. Toddlers have undeveloped vocal cords and have not yet begun to formulate sounds into meaningful words. Speech, which is really a combination of mental and physical processes, will come eventually. At this age, parents can help a child with musical sounds and rhythm. Parents can do the singing. Let the child bang on a block, use some sort of rhythm instrument, or clap his or her hands along with the parents.

Energy Level. Most preschoolers tire easily. They cannot maintain an enriched stimulus for more than a few minutes. This is the case for two reasons. First, they simply get stimuli overload. Various stimuli are not "old hat," as they would be for older children. For the preschooler, the world is new every day and often every moment.

Second, preschoolers do not have much energy storage capacity. Their little bodies are using up most of their energy to develop physically. There is so much developing internally, such as organs, muscles, tissue, blood, etc., that takes their energy to stay alive and grow. So they simply run out of steam after a short while. If parents or older siblings play too long with early preschoolers, and even older preschoolers, they can easily tire them out and make them susceptible to illness. Parents need to alternate between active and quiet activities, as well as to provide a variety of activities.

It is typical for a parent to return from work and provide a preschooler with lots of activities—running, playing, reading—things that the parent wishes they could have done all day with the child. But the child gets tired and/or bored quickly. Often parents think that they have done something wrong or that there is something wrong with their child, or that their child is not having a good experience in day care. While sickness and improper day care might be a problem and should not be minimized, the chances are that the child is just being overstimulated and is tired. Parents of preschoolers need to remember to treat their children as preschoolers, not junior highers!

Older Preschoolers
Later preschool-age children—ages three-and-a-half to about five—continue to develop much as they did in their earlier years, only not as rapidly. They still tire easily but do have more stamina. Their attention spans are a bit longer, though they continue to lack the attention of an elementary-age child. Actually, their total physical development will not be completed until their mid-to-late twenties! It is no wonder, then, that children and youth tire easily. They never seem to stop growing!

Older preschoolers have greater muscle dexterity, but still lack the fine muscle development of older children. Don't expect a three-year-old to match Johann Sebastian Bach's fine finger dexterity on the piano. Still, whereas a one-year-old might not be able to turn a page in a book, a four-year-old not only can turn pages, but can easily recognize when the book is upside down. There is such a large amount of development that occurs in these early years that most parents marvel at the physical growth that is occurring.

Notice Little Changes. Parents need to be sensitive to the development of their children. It should not come as any great surprise that a child sometimes seems to have grown noticeably in one day while the parents were at work. Small changes should be noted, especially when the child is eager to show the parents some newly developed action. Take time to receive such revelations, provide lots of praise, and ask the child to repeat the new action as often as the child might want to do so (given a reasonable number of repetitions!). The parent will become bored more readily than a child. Try to remember your own excitement with a newfound affection or "toy." Our children are no different. We need to encourage them and even help the child to perfect that particular behavior.

Differences. Remember that individual differences occur between siblings and not just between children of different families. Parents should not measure one child against another in the family. One child will develop more quickly in one area of physical development than a brother or sister or relative. Our two children both walked at ten months. They have a cousin who did not walk until he was almost two years old. All were normal. They simply had different timetables. Our two children were "potty trained" by about twenty-four months. One cousin absolutely refused to be toilet-trained and told his mother that in no uncertain terms. He decided he would use the toilet on his third birthday and he did, much to the relief of his very frustrated parents.

Early Elementary Age

Around five years of age preschoolers experience a lull in their rapid development. Beginning around age six, they begin to again develop rapidly. As in the preceding years, however, early elementary children's growth is uneven. Heart and lungs do not keep pace with the rest of the large muscles and skeletal growth. Small muscles that were once difficult to control are now developing. Yet those small muscles can tire easily. Thus they need only short periods of small muscle activity—five to eight minutes rather than a half-hour or more. Still, the young child does need to have plenty of opportunities to use his or her small muscles. Wise parents will use those short moments before and after work to ask their child to show them how he or she can write (or to do some other activity that requires newly acquired small muscle dexterity).

Early elementary children are, like their earlier counterparts, susceptible to contagious diseases. Colds, flu, measles, and other common childhood diseases are easily passed from one child to another. And, unfortunately, passed to the parents as well.

Children of early elementary age are active and like strenuous activities that stretch their abilities without over-stressing them. They like to put on "shows" for their parents and anyone who will watch. The wise parent encourages a certain amount of "show and tell" at home instead of just at school. Children need to be able to express themselves in actions and spontaneous programs for their parents' benefit.

Working parents can show their understanding of their early elementary children's growth by helping them to learn to do things that they have the capability to do but lack the knowledge of how to do them. The idea is to help one's children use their bodies in constructive ways that will help the busy working family. For example, show them an "older person's" job such as raking the yard or taking out the trash. Help them to learn the most effective and efficient way to do it and then give them the job when you feel that they can accomplish it in a reasonably satisfactory manner.

Older Elementary Age
Older elementary children, usually considered to be around ages eight or nine through eleven, are full of energy. The sturdy health and seemingly endless energy of this age-group means that they are in constant motion, looking for things to keep their now seemingly well-developed child's body moving. Their fine muscles are well coordinated and they continually refine skills that require increasingly more fine muscle control. They pay attention, generally, to details and can be counted on to notice a great many more details than they would have as recently as age seven.

Athletic activities become more and more important for American children in this age-group. Even while children are in late preschool, parents can help them begin to enjoy sports activities. This is not for competition's sake, but for learning physical coordination skills and how to interact with others.

Along with teaching your children how to play a game, you can also begin to teach them how to lose at a competitive game without also losing their self-esteem. (Part of the problem in teaching children this is that many parents have yet to figure it out for themselves!) Children need to learn that playing fairly and up to their abilities is what counts; winning is nice, but not necessary to having fun and to being accepted by one's parents. Encourage your children to play hard and well, learning all the time how to become more adept in their athletic skill without being overly concerned about winning or losing.

Some girls begin their sexual development at age eleven, and a few even at ten. Parents need to be ready to discuss with their daughters what is about to happen or has already begun to happen to their bodies. Boys' sexual development does not normally begin until their adolescent years. However, it is not too early to lay the basic groundwork of trust and love for children of both sexes to talk about sexual development during this late elementary age. They're seeing it on television and hearing about it at school at this age. It is very important for the busy parent to take extra time for this, even if it means giving up something else.

Working parents should look for active things to do with their children. Fathers can take a few minutes before or after the evening meal to throw a ball or Frisbee with their children. Weekends can be used for some more special activities like a bike ride or picnic. These weekend events do not have to consume the whole day. A few hours of biking and picnicking can make a big difference in how children respond to their parents, not only during their elementary years but also in their teenage years. Parents are establishing all along that they are interested in their children, will meet them at their developmental level, and will continue to be committed to them.

Early Adolescence
Early adolescence (ages twelve to fourteen) is marked with a dramatic change in physical development. Whereas in childhood boys and girls were developing at more or less the same rate, now girls are far ahead of boys. It will not be until mid-to-late

high school years that boys become stronger and larger than girls.

From a physical perspective the onset of adolescence starts with the secretion of the pituitary gland, which begins sexual development and the completion of physical development. Parents have only to remember the painful days of their junior high years to recall the physical changes that occurred in that formative time. Adolescents are moving from a child's body to an adult body, but they do so in fits and starts. Girls develop earlier and soon make the boys look like children. Boys eventually will catch up, but suffer the sense of being smaller, weaker, and less coordinated than girls almost all of their early adolescent years.

Girls' Development. Girls develop sexually with the onset of menarche. This is a most crucial period when a mother or other trusted adult woman can be of great help for a young woman to understand how her body works. The sensitive and wise mother takes the time needed to help her daughter know what will happen to her body long before it happens. Talks at night at bedtime or while watching a TV advertisement for women's sanitary products can be natural times and places for this discussion to begin. If a daughter doesn't bring it up, the mother should!

Boys' Development. Early adolescent boys are more akin to late childhood boys than to adolescents. They are behind in physical development, size, and strength compared to their female agemates. This situation makes boys feel insecure around their female friends and often drives them to friendships only with the boys. All the while they are beginning to look with a strange longing, but lack of understanding, at their female classmates.

Boys usually begin their adolescent physical development about one to two years behind girls. When they do begin, they often experience short spurts of physical growth. Our son grew six inches in one year. Skeletal growth (bones) seems to far outstrip muscle growth and both skeletal and muscle growth far surpass boys' abilities to control their bodies. Awkwardness is not unusual at this age.

At some point between ages twelve and fourteen, the boys

begin their sexual development. These changes in a boy's development are accompanied by the same type of questions that girls have about their physical development.

Talking to Your Adolescents about Their Bodies. Early adolescent youth are plagued with questions about their physical development. It is almost universal in our world that younger adolescent youth have an ideal picture of what it means to be a man or woman. That ideal is based almost entirely on what they have seen in the mass media.

Youth of this age-group know more about physical development than any other part of their growth and development, yet they are woefully ignorant of what it really means to begin to have an adult body. They need to know that their bodies are not misfits. Explain to them that their bodies are not necessarily finished yet—in fact, they will probably not be for another decade. But they do need to know how to take care of those bodies, how to enhance their development, and how to protect their bodies against experimentation that could do serious damage and from unscrupulous people who would use their bodies for their own selfish and sinful ends.

Wise parents also will begin to bring in spiritual values about one's body. Discuss such things as how our bodies are God's temple, and that He indwells us. And therefore we must take care of our bodies and not defile them any more than we would want to rip up the hymnbooks or write nasty words all over our church's walls.

Boys and girls both need to know that the sexes are God-given and that being male or female is to be used for His glory and not just for our pleasure. But God *has* intended sexuality for us humans for our pleasure. Sex is not bad; it is often misused, however. Whether it is good or bad depends on who uses it for what and when and with whom. These are values, not just knowledge of physical functioning. Wise (though busy) parents find times and occasions to bring up sexuality and to teach the values as well as functions of sexuality. Those sex education classes often begun in public or private schools in the mid-to-late elementary grades offer a springboard for discussion. Take the time to ask what was taught, how the child felt about it, what they he or she didn't understand, and what questions he or she might have as a result of those experiences.

Middle Adolescence
Middle adolescence covers the ages of fifteen through eighteen. During this time both male and female bodies continue to develop into increasingly more adult forms. Sexual development is almost complete, if not completed, during this time. Physical development in its largest areas of muscles and bone growth is almost complete. A few facial bones and some neurological growth will continue into the college-age years of late adolescence.

While early adolescents tire more quickly, middle adolescents have more stamina. Middle adolescents are more coordinated, especially the boys, in comparison to their earlier adolescent years. Sexually, they are for the most part mature and capable of having children, as is proven far too often each year.

Taking Care of the Adolescent Body. In spite of their physical development to almost adult size and proportions, middle adolescents face the same questions as in early adolescence: How will I control this body? How will I make this body work properly? How will I keep this body functioning well? Parents who are wise and sensitive will take opportunities to talk with their teenagers about the care and feeding of their bodies.

Youth are easily led into believing that if they feel well-fed with junk food they are eating well. They need to know about nutrition, exercise, and proper sleep habits. Unfortunately, their parents often are having the same battle as the children. The workplace is not always conducive to healthy living for parents. If this is the case, then why not suggest a family conversation on how *we*, not just the kids, can control eating, appetites, and exercise. Parents and kids can become accountable to each other rather than just kids to parents. A new level of camaraderie will be developed as parents and kids struggle together to help each other become successful in the maintenance of their physical selves. Parents can achieve a weight that they need, eat a more healthful diet, and thus stave off heart and other vital organ problems, and kids learn good health habits to develop strong bodies that will continue into adulthood.

A mutual physical development program does not have to become a major issue in the family. As kids mention the need to diet, drink protein, or work out, parents can join in and suggest that they need this too. You don't have to do it together, but can agree on parallel programs. Check in with each other's progress weekly, holding each other accountable for goals set, rewarding each other, and occasionally having a family celebration after passing some major milestone.

Conclusion

The physical development of middle adolescents can and ought to be part of the whole of a family's perspective. Physical growth of the child is not easy to keep secret: kids just get bigger. And accompanying this "bigness" are all the aspects of sexual maturing and increases of strength that are parts of the process. Parents who excitedly share in their children's physical growth, and who can appreciate that growth and help their children accept what God is doing in their bodies, can become increasingly more effective parents.

COGNITIVE DEVELOPMENT

Children think! Not like adults, like children. Just how do they think like children?

It goes without saying that the cognitive or mental processes of an infant are very limited. We have yet to determine that an infant thinks in any way similar to the older child of five or six. But an infant does have cognitive processes at work. These processes that God has placed within each child will continue to develop until the helpless infant who has only a very basic cognitive process is able to think the deep, abstract thoughts of a philosopher.

The cognitive processes are important because they become the foundation for four remaining developmental processes. Just as the cognitive process will not develop if the brain does not mature, so social, emotional (affective), moral, and spiritual development will not occur unless the child develops in his or her mental processes.

Cognitive development has been analyzed into four stages by the noted developmentalist Jean Piaget.[1] The four stages of cognitive development are *sensori-motor* (sensory and acting), *pre-operational, concrete operations,* and *formal operations.*

Stage One—Sensing and Acting
This stage is characterized by a different type of "thinking" than most adults are familiar with. Sensori-motor children process their environmental stimuli through three things: (1) movements and actions, (2) general perceptions achieved by sensory experiences, and (3) direct actions on the reality that surrounds them. They do not use words to represent things.

For most children in this stage, when an object or person is removed from their sight, they do not think that the object or person still exists. For all that the child knows, the object or person has permanently disappeared. The child will have a memory of the object or person, but he or she will not think that its existence continues when the child can no longer sense it.

Children at this stage—from brith to about two or two-and-one-half years of age—center their thoughts on themselves. The whole world is limited to what *they* can perceive. Until the latter part of this stage, there is no language.

How Busy Parents Can Help Sensori-Motor Children Develop.
Children at this age can be helped to develop by giving them a rich environment full of various stimuli which they can perceive. Just a simple drawing or a melody line of some music is all that children of this stage will make sense of cognitively, not the fine details that often are found in some art for children.They cannot take in the subtleties of fine art, or even chords in hymns, choruses, and other music.

Parents can read simple stories with very limited plots and with plenty of simple pictures to illustrate the story. It does not take much time to go through a couple of these types of books geared to the sensori-motor child—books that allow a child to feel, smell, scratch, look, and hear are ideal. Parents who understand that their children's world is limited to what the children perceive will fill that world with pleasant experiences and with appropriate stimuli to broaden the world.

Children at this stage cannot participate "passively" in anything. They need to have a "hands on" approach to the world around them, to touch, taste, see, feel, hear, and smell things. Ideas as abstract entities that reside in our adult minds do not exist for children in this stage. Their world is limited to the sensori and motor—to the five senses and to actions with one or more of their five senses.

A sensori-motor child will grasp a toy and after feeling it for a brief moment, will stick it in his or her mouth. How else could he or she know what the toy is, unless it is checked out by sight, touch, and taste! As many real things as possible should be given to the child to play with and to experiment with through his or her sensori-motor actions. Repetition of sounds and experiences makes children in this stage happy. They can predict what will come next and that gives them a sense of control over their limited world.

As already mentioned, do not be surprised that the attention span of a sensori-motor child is short, lasting about two to three minutes with the occasional attention span of four minutes. Thus parents need to keep one step ahead of their sensori-motor stage child with books, toys, actions, and experiences that can be changed every few minutes and then repeated again several times over. Usually parents will become bored long before the child does.

Working parents of sensori-motor stage children can easily show love to their children after work with hugs and kisses and by providing activities for the child as the child sits on Mommy's or Daddy's lap. A child "feels" love from the sense of physical closeness to his or her parent and from being able to become actively involved in what the parent is doing with the child. On the way home from day care, a parent can bring a toy for the child to play with, perhaps a favorite stuffed animal or something that the child likes to chew on or look at—something bright and interesting.

Talking about God. Parents can teach about God with sensori-motor experiences, rather than with concepts. For example, when a parent and child see a pretty color, they can thank God for making pretty colors. When they see an animal that the child likes, they can thank God for it. When the parent tries to teach that "God is love," he or she should do it with a hug and a statement that God loves you and so do Daddy and Mommy, and then give a kiss and another hug.

Parents should not be too surprised when they find that their children in this stage are not interested in Bible verses, family devotions, hymn singing, or worship services; they do not perceive much of what adults can from these experiences.

Stage Two—Pre-Operational Stage

In Stage Two, children are able to make a distinction between objects or events and the words that represent them. In other words, children know the difference between a mental idea—a word—and the actual thing that the word stands for. Thus the word "chair" means something to children at this stage, whereas in the sensori-motor stage it was just a sound without any mental concept.

Language and speech begin in earnest now. Children are able to communicate with words and ideas, though their definitions are functional, not abstract. For example, when asked, "What is a fork?" most children at this stage will state something like, "A fork is for eating," rather than giving a more abstract definition such as, "A fork is a three-or-four-pronged, hand-held instrument used in many cultures for placing food in one's mouth." As in the sensori-motor stage, these children tie thinking to action. They reason from one particular thing or event to another. Often they connect each thing to everything else. It is not unusual for children of this stage to think that inanimate objects such as dolls, teddy bears, etc. have their own life.

Inside the Pre-Operational Mind. Thinking for children in this stage is limited to what can be perceived through their senses. They are unable to distinguish between their own thoughts and those of others.

Children of this stage will often give reasons for their beliefs and actions. But they do not make comparisons nor are they able to hold in their minds more than one concrete item or concept at a time.

They can follow a line of reasoning from beginning to end, but they cannot reverse the line of thought and rethink the whole process from the end back to the beginning. They center their focus of thinking on fixed perceived stimuli. They cannot figure out how what they see got the way it is.

For example, suppose you show a child at this stage two containers—one long and flat (like a glass baking dish) and the other, tall. Then you measure a quart of water into a pitcher and pour the water into the flat container, repeating the same thing with the tall container. If you ask the child which of the now-filled containers has the most water, he or she will choose one or the other, but not both. Why? Because the child centers his or her thoughts on the shape of the container and not on the quart pitcher from which the water was poured. The child has focused on one action and idea and cannot operate mentally on the observations that he or she experienced. The child takes the experiences just as they come and as he or she observes them. A child at this stage is perception bound, that is, he or she cannot think beyond what is experienced. A child in this stage, there-fore, thinks and has ideas but is limited to the world that he or she can perceive with one or more senses.

Helping the Pre-Operational Child to Develop. Parents who are wise and effective will provide stimuli to help their children think about the real world. The stimuli need to be simple, separate, and within the child's experiences. Since pre-operational children's physical actions cause them to think, parents need to provide plenty of action. Watching TV is not a way to stimulate thinking unless parents watch it with their children and ask questions such as, "Why did the man do that to the other person?" or, "Why did that happen to her?" and so forth.

When parents return from work and are with their children at night or on weekends or vacation days, they should ask the children to tell them about their day at school, the day-care center, or with the baby-sitter. Parents should continue not only to listen but also to elicit meaning from their children by asking questions such as, "Why do you think that is so good?" or, "Why did Bobby get into trouble at school?" or, "What was the best part of school today?" or, "Why did you like that story your teacher read to you?"

The general idea is to help children think through the concrete, discrete, individual events and experiences of their day, to share those events and experiences from their perspective, and to help the children make meaning or express the meaning of those events and experiences. The time involved to do this is not much—a few minutes around the dinner table, just before being tucked into bed at night, or when the child arrives home and is ready to unload all the things that were meaningful to him or her that day.

Stage Three—Concrete Operations

This stage generally begins around ages seven or eight and can continue throughout adulthood. It is one where the thinking of children, and many adults, is limited to concrete things: events, experiences, persons, etc. Much like the children in Stage Two, these children cannot think abstractly. Philosophy and theology are not understood; algebra, calculus, and even geometry do not make much sense. In fact, children in concrete operations not only would not understand what was being taught, but they would also probably totally misunderstand.

Children in the concrete operational stage are able to think about many things simultaneously as long as they are limited to the real or concrete world. Whereas the pre-operational child could not follow an argument from its end back to its beginning, a concrete thinker now can. Children in this stage can solve problems in their heads and have a very large capacity to think. But, again, they think about things that are real and available to their senses and not about abstract ideas.

Concepts like "truth," "love," or "redemption" can be memorized and even used in a sentence, but a concrete thinker will not understand them in their fullness. Concrete-thinking children only have a very vague feeling about some of these important concepts, caught from the way their parents and other significant people in their lives respond to the concepts. These children, however, can and do understand these and many other concepts in their concrete applications. So it is not meaningless to talk about truth in terms of telling the truth—to tell it exactly as it really happened, not as you would like it to have happened. Arithmetic is achievable for children in this stage whereas algebra is not. The experiment with the water in two different containers which was described under Stage Two no longer confuses concrete thinkers. They are able to keep in mind both the volume and shapes of containers and are not confused by the changing shape. Again, what is concrete or real they can understand and can think about.

Helping Your Concrete Operational Child to Develop. Working parents of children in this stage can continue to ask questions about the experiences of their children during the day. Expect concrete responses and descriptions of what happened and why. Continue to provide plenty of opportunities for discussion of the day's experiences and seek to find out what sense your children have made of them.

Children can also have enriched interaction with the real world through trips, videos, books, magazines, and other vicarious experiences. Weekend, vacation time, and after-school experiences can be planned by parents to provide continued input for the concrete minds of their children. Just having a variety of good magazines around the house will provide opportunity for children to look at concrete realities in different settings.

Children should be shown how valuable their school, community, and church libraries are. Beginning with age four or five (and even at age three for some), take your children to the library and show them the books and videos that they can choose to check out and use at home.

Sitting with your children for even five minutes after dinner to look at a book or magazine and talk about what they see and what it means to them will give tremendous stimuli to continue looking and reading on their own. This also sends a message to the children that it is important to read and be acquainted with the world around them and all its different people, places, and events.

Stage Four—Formal Operations

Stage Four does not begin until usually about age twelve or later. Many adults—one writer stated 50 percent of adults—do not ever achieve this stage of cognitive development. And many children do not achieve a functioning formal or abstract thinking ability until mid-to-late high school.

Verbal problems, logic, algebra, calculus, philosophy, and theology and the abstract ideas that go along with these are all able to be used by persons in this fourth stage of thinking. Whereas the concrete thinker could only focus on concrete ideas and the pre-operational thinker could only focus on what he or she could perceive, this person can think about abstract ideas or inferences that are not at all real and may not ever be.

One should not misunderstand the abstract thinker as a dreamer. Rather, abstract or formal operations thinkers are people who have the full repertoire of all the other stages that they have gone through, along with this new stage of thinking about what might be. One person characterized this stage person as "thinking about thinking."

Helping Your Formal Operational Child to Develop. Wise and effective parents of abstract thinkers continue to dialogue with their children. But now the focus is not what their experience was or a description of an event. Rather it is to explore the future with your children, to ask "Why?" and "Why not?" questions, to examine possibilities and new meanings. Questions and dialogue are now the ways for parents to interact with their children.

This sort of dialogue—not just questions and answers, but mutual sharing of ideas and dreams—will take more time than that necessary with pre-operational or concrete thinking children. Now the adult parent is talking with, not to, a child who has adult thinking capabilities. The parent is helping the children to engage in an "adults only" activity: to think abstractly about the future and its meaning for now and later. Parents who do these sorts of activities with their children find that they learn much about what is going on in their children's minds and get to know their children on a deeper and more intimate level. Children whose parents talk with them on this abstract level also get to know their parents not so much as providers or disciplinarians, but as human beings who also think!

Conclusion

We have seen in this chapter how infants quickly begin their development. They move from total physical dependence on parents to the almost fully physically mature teenager. And we have discussed the four stages of mental development, from being limited to sensory and motor experiences to eventually being able to think like a philosopher or theologian. From infancy to late adolescence is a long way to go in a *very* short period of years. Busy, working parents, who understand their child's development, can use their time more effectively and purposefully.

Check up on your child/children's development and your observations.

Fill out the sheet individually. If you are married share your answers with your spouse.

Describe each of your children in the two developmental areas that follow. Then add what their development would suggest that they need from you as a parent. List at least six to eight characteristics in each developmental area and at least an equal number in the developmental needs column. (You may want to review each section of this chapter to see some of the major developmental changes that take place in children.)

Physical development characteristics	*Developmental needs for parent(s) to supply*

Cognitive development characteristics	*Developmental needs for parent(s) to supply*

Six.
Learning to Live
with Others

Even in the crib nursery at church, infants will look at each other. Probably the first emotion an infant has is the response to a slap on the bottom at birth. From birth on, children are social and emotional beings. Normal parents want their children to develop social skills, and rightly so. But social skills demonstrate what is inside—social development. It is the movement from less to more mature in social developmental areas that will affect how well children fit into their various social contexts. The first part of this chapter deals with social development.

Affective (psychological or emotional) development is the second developmental area that we will focus on. The area of the emotions and feelings is undoubtedly the least understood developmental area. Both social and emotional growth are so important—working parents must take the time to understand how their child is maturing.

SOCIAL DEVELOPMENT

Social development seems to be almost a fetish with middle and upper class parents and is increasingly becoming an issue with lower class parents as well. Parents want their children to "fit in" with their friends and not be socially isolated. Our American school systems reinforce and sometimes even lead in this area of "fitting in" with others, and social conformity rather than personal individuality is stressed.

Neither the social nor the emotional development areas have neat little stages that easily describe what to expect as children move from less to more mature. There are, however, some major social developmental accomplishments that we can see as children grow from infancy through adolescence. These follow within age-group breakdowns.

Young Preschoolers

Children of this age are egocentric (in a positive sense) — at this time their social world is defined only by themselves. It comes to them through their sensori-motor perceptions, through their five senses. Thus they know the world of social relationships through a very narrow channel which does not give them a very broad perspective.

The infant is unaware that there are ongoing relationships around him or her. As they grow from the first few months of life to their second year of life, infants begin to realize that reality exists apart from them. This reality includes the fact that others exist after they leave the room, and that relationships they have with parents and others do not cease and begin anew each time that person reenters his or her environment.

Younger preschoolers are self-centered and possessive. Sharing is not a natural trait with them. Their world revolves around themselves and they do not yet know how to relate to an external world of social relationships. It is not unusual to have several preschoolers in the same room playing by themselves. They play parallel to each other, but not with each other. They do, however, imitate what they see in social relationships. It is not unusual for a preschooler to express "No!" very forcefully, as if to say to his or her parents and other caregivers, "I have my *own* identity!" Yet preschoolers are open to suggestions, generally cooperative, and relatively eager to please.

Wise and effective parents of preschoolers seek to help their children build on the limited social development of their first few years of life. Do not be surprised by egocentric behavior or interpret their self-centeredness as a sure sign of original sin. Rather, realize that your children's lives are centered on only what they know, namely, their own narrow world. Begin to help your children have experiences with others which will help them realize that their world is broader than their preschool minds. Help your younger preschoolers to notice other children, older or younger, and adults, expressing happiness at seeing them.

Older Preschoolers

As children reach older preschool years, they begin to realize that the world is greater than their limited perception. Other people do matter and there is a give-and-take in social relationships. Getting along with others is important—there are ways and means of sharing oneself and possessions that make for two happy children instead of just "myself."

Older preschoolers have a developing vocabulary and use it in many social situations. The greater their vocabulary and the more their families encourage verbal expression, the more they will talk with just about anyone about whatever they know. This increase in vocabulary and desire to practice it can be used by parents to elicit comments about their children's experiences at the day-care center or baby-sitter's. Children like to use new-found abilities, and parents need to help them find opportunities to use them. Asking your children how the day went, what they did, who did what, when, etc. are all ways to help children continue their social development and to use their vocabulary.

Wise and effective parents will ask "Why?" questions rather than only factual ones. "Why" questions require the children to process the information and not merely repeat facts. Of course, parents should not expect a well-thought-out rationale in response to "why" questions. Remember, preschoolers *are still* preschoolers, not adult philosophers.

Working parents can ask "Why?" questions—at home during breakfast, on the way to day care and on the way back, at home at night, just before bedtime, and all weekend long. It will not be too many years before the children themselves, now older, will be asking *you* the "Why?" and "Why not?" questions about almost anything.

Elementary Age

Children of school age often are found in informal, unorganized, or at best relatively disorganized social groups or gangs. These are informal gatherings of children of the same age and sex for play.

Children are conscious that others are aware of them, but they do not make decisions or take actions based on that knowledge. Being looked at by others does not affect their actions in a social situation. Later in this elementary period, children begin to realize that they are being viewed by others and they will actually try to see themselves from the other's perspective. This form of social perspective is very crucial for the development of conscious empathy, which we talk about in the affective development area of this chapter.

Hero worship is a major part of social development for elementary children. Heroes vary from child to child and from year to year. Because children of this age have heroes, they also imitate those whom they look up to. Adults and biblical characters can be important teachers when it comes to helping this age-group of children know how to act in social settings.

Elementary children pick up the emphasis on competition from their major culture. Like ducks to water, many will become very competitive. Because most younger elementary children are on an equal status when it comes to the majority of competition, none of them are hurt by losing. They may lose today, but tomorrow they will win. Usually no one has the decisive edge either physically or in other areas at age six or seven. Children naturally desire to excel and willingly enter into competition whether it be in the classroom or in sports activities.

By the third grade this equality is erased and children continue to excel or lose consistently in one or more areas. Soon competition is predictable: the same one or two children will win the spelling contest every time. Parents may want to suggest that teachers use something in addition to competition to stimulate interest in education and sports.

Elementary children become more self-assertive and take responsibilities in many areas of their lives. They enjoy having their own tasks to do and will respond eagerly if they feel that their job is appreciated. Working parents can use this interest in responsibility to give their children their own tasks to complete. Children can begin to do relatively simple tasks at ages six and seven and eventually will handle more complex and responsible tasks. *Caution.* Be sure to teach your children how to do their tasks before asking them to do them on their own.

Safety Rules When Parents Are Absent — Elementary Age. Often older elementary (and even younger elementary) age children arrive home to an empty house — they are called "latchkey" children. They need to know the behavior allowed and disallowed in the time between their arrival from school and the parents' arrival from work. Activities and houseguests need to be regulated, and children need to know definite limits to each. Can a friend come in to use the bathroom? Have some cookies and milk? Play a video game? Can friends of the opposite sex come into the house? Can the child cook something on the stove or in the microwave oven? What things do they have to do immediately upon getting home: call a parent, let out the dog, chores, homework, practice music?

Rules for children need to be made by the parents and explained to the children. The children cannot always follow the reasoning of adults (until about age ten or eleven), but they do need to know that rules are not merely arbitrary edicts from the more powerful parent to the children. They need to see that rules are for their benefit and that breaking them has its consequences, while keeping them offers some additional rewards.

Adolescent Years
Youth often "hang around" in small groups. These start with superficial peer groups made up of a conglomeration of all types

of friends in junior high, and eventually develop in the late high school and early college years into small, intimate groups. As youth become more mature in other areas of their lives, they begin to make and keep friends who have similar interests. Youth, regardless of their age, are usually loyal to their peers and especially to their group. They are peer-oriented and pick up the values of the group with which they hang out. They have conflicting social impulses to be loyal and helpful and also at the same time to be self-centered. Youth need direction to take their minds off of themselves. They need help in recognizing that they have responsibilities for living with the family and in their relationships with others at school. They continue to worship heroes, but now it is most often popular music, TV, or movie personalities. However, it is not unusual to find that parents are part of the adolescent's list of "people whom I most admire."

Social-Sexual Development. Crushes, romance, falling in love, and sexual experimentation take place from junior high age on. The whole area of sexual development is probably one of the greatest uncertainties for both the adolescents and their parents. Often parents are reticent to talk to their adolescent children about sex and its meaning and the biblical values associated with sex. Yet their children are ignorant of some of the most basic data about sex, even after school sex education classes. They are certainly almost totally ignorant about biblical sexual values and morality.

"Just say no," borrowed from the anti-drug campaign, may work for a seventy-five-year-old woman, but it does not sound like a great solution to a bunch of adolescents who are filled with curiosity and sexual drives. They need help in understanding their sexual development and its meaning in their lives as Christians. With soap operas on TV in the afternoon, cable TV, videos, and a flood of magazines for both males and females to look at, adolescents today are surfeited with sex. Today's teens do not need parents who preach at them. What they do need are wise and understanding parents who ask questions, make suggestions, turn their children's minds to why God created male and female, and tell them how to control their God-given sex drives.

Setting Rules When Parents Are Absent—Teenage Years. When working parents are absent for a good part of the afternoon each weekday and are gone all day during the summer months, these parents need to make sure that their children are aware of expected behavior at home. Review each day's scheduled activities with your teenagers either the night before or at breakfast to be sure that what is expected will be performed appropriately. Rules as to who may enter the house and what activities are allowed when parents are not at home should be agreed on. Expect them to be followed without serious deviation.

It is important that rules be discussed with teenagers, not imposed from above without explanation and mutual agreement. Imposed rules are merely an invitation to find ways and means to break them. Mutually agreed on rules set an expectation that makes deviation a much more serious result for the inner psyche of the teenager. The teenager has been part of the rule-making process, has understood the reasoning behind the rules, and has given his or her consent to the rules. Utlimately, the teenager has made a commitment to what is agreed on as the right thing to do. Deviation from such commitments is much more difficult for everyone involved.

Nearly Adults. Throughout the teenage years, youth feel as if they are neither children nor adults. They want to be grown-up yet they do not want to leave childhood and all its ease and security behind. Socially, the move from childhood to adulthood is a difficult one. It seems to adolescents that everyone is looking at them: at their physical growth, at their speaking in public with others, at their way of responding to questions—at *everything* they do. They start experimenting with different personality traits. Seemingly, they try on a new personality identity or trait every week or so to see how their friends and family and teachers will react.

Youth look for models to copy when it comes to social skills and social roles. They will do as their parents do when they meet people and they will function as they have been taught in the social roles that they play. Fortunately, as youth grow from early to middle adolescence they are less self-focused and more focused on others. They are able to get along with different people and can and will carry on an adult-like conversation with someone older. Throughout adolescence and well into adulthood, most youth want to be liked by others. They want to be popular with some group and to feel that they have a place and role in society that is greater and more important than just attending school every day.

Wise and effective parents will treat their teenagers as nearly adults, not as changing children. This requires a major shift in how parents value and deal with their adolescent children. The shift does not come overnight, but takes a conscious effort on the part of parents to no longer think of "my child" but of "my almost-young-adult, no-longer-a-child." Give them social roles to fill in the home and with the family as a way to help them become socially adept and to have confidence in their own social development. Asking one's son or daughter to order for the family at a restaurant is a major step for the young person as well as for the parents. Helping them prepare interesting questions to ask company or relatives is another way to encourage this social development.

In the end, social development is one of the most externally observable means for your offspring to show that he or she is no longer a child but has "grown up" and is now capable of existing effectively in an adult world.

AFFECTIVE DEVELOPMENT

Emotions, feelings, desires, and the will comprise the affective development area. When we have feelings, and then examine these feelings or determine to act on them, we use our cognitive or mental developmental aspects of personhood. The emotions and thinking interact.

Behavior, therefore, is neither purely rational nor purely affective; it is a combination of both. We like something, we reflect on its likability, we determine to do something, we make plans to do it, and then we do it. All of these internal activities that lead to the actual behavior are a combination of the thinking area and the feeling area. While we can logically separate these two processes from each other in order to examine them, in reality they are one continuous process. We do not feel, then think, then feel, then think. It happens seemingly as a whole. We need to look at this area of development because from it and in it come the seeds of all sorts of actions.

Affective development does not fit into neat stages or levels of development. From the earliest age, children experience joy, happiness, pleasure, displeasure, sadness, anger, fear, anxiety, shock, hostility, and a whole host of other emotions that adults also experience.

Adults can define and explain, and even share their emotional feelings with another; children and many adolescents cannot. But they can experience the emotion, show the emotion, and know that they are having that particular emotion. So it is normal for children to have emotions, but they most likely are unable to handle those emotions in a so-called "mature" manner as adults would. They are not mature. They are not adults. They are children or adolescents and thus feel and act less mature!

Teaching Expression of Emotions

Families, especially parents, tend to teach what emotions are expressible and how they can be expressed. Parents teach their children that some emotions may not be expressed to others outside the family, some emotions can be expressed inside the family's house, and others can never be expressed anywhere. One woman we know told us that her parents very carefully instructed her as to which emotions she could show in public.

From the earliest days of life on, parents teach which emotions are OK to show. When a child smiles or acts happy, parents will smile back, repeating the emotion back to the child. But when the child acts sad or angry, the parent will either ignore the emotion or will try to change the emotion to a positive and therefore acceptable one. Children soon learn that negative emotions are not acceptable and positive ones are. As children grow older, parents tell them directly which emotions are acceptable to show and which are not.

Working with Your Child's Emotions

Wise and effective parents recognize their children's emotions, and work with their children during the highs and lows of those emotional experiences. The goal of wise and effective parenting is not to extinguish the children's emotions but to help children develop healthy emotions and a healthy means of expressing those emotions. Both healthy emotions and healthy expressions are key to emotionally well-developed children.

Not only do parents need to recognize that their children have emotions, but they also need to recognize when they are having particular emotions. John recalls that his father recognized the fact that when at age five or six he would hear a scary story just before bedtime, he would have "bad dreams" that night. His father suggested two things: One was "do not listen to scary stories on the radio just before you go to bed." Number two was that "those are just stories, just make-believe things that did not happen. They are not real, so what is not real cannot scare you in your reality." John chose the second alternative, not wanting to give up those fascinating stories on the radio!

When parents recognize their children's emotions, they can then assist them by helping to identify the emotions for them. Share in the child's emotions by saying, "I had that same feeling when I was your age . . . " or something else that suggests that the parent has been there already.

Parents can also realize that there are emotions in many settings and experiences of their children's daily lives. Books, TV programs, audio tapes, games, and the daily interpersonal encounters with family, friends, and the general public all have weak to strong emotional content. It is these many and varied experiences of daily living that parents can and should use to help their children to mature emotionally.

Often, in middle and upper class societies, emotions are suppressed and a bland social self is expressed—one does not show emotions in "polite society." It is ultimately destructive for a child to learn this. Emotions need to be expressed and always will be in one way or another. They will either be expressed in a healthy or unhealthy manner, or will be repressed and expressed in ways that confuse child, parents, and the rest of society.

Carrying unresolved anger overtime or just into the night (Eph. 4:26) means that our minds dwell on it, our subconscious thoughts still wrestle with our anger, and our physical bodies are still ready to do battle with whatever caused that anger. This will do untold damage to our hearts, souls, minds, and bodies. It is the unhealthy way of dealing with the emotion that causes the damage, not the emotion itself.

Busy parents need to help their children each night to deal with any negative emotions they may have experienced that day. The moments at bedtime when a parent prays with the child are a good time to talk to God about the emotions of the day and the anger, fear, resentment, jealousies, or other negative emotions that are still in the mind. Just telling God about these feelings will help the child, and the parent, to rest on and in God.

Bedtime is also a good time to tell God how happy one is. The time at the close of the day can and should become a final wrap-up of the emotional ups and downs that one has experienced. But the positive feelings of the day need to be expressed along with the negatives. Remember, your child had a full day of emotions while you were at work. Help them to unburden their negatives and help them to rejoice in their positives. Help them to see that God loves us regardless of our emotional states. His love does not go up and down. He is always loving.

Psychological Development

Eight stages of psychological or affective development have been identified by the renowned psychologist Erik H. Erikson.[1] The first four stages deal with children and Stage Five deals with youth. Stages Six, Seven, and Eight are adult stages and will not be included.

In Stage One — *Basic Trust vs. Basic Mistrust* — infants learn to trust that their mother and other caregivers will not disappear. Infants can count on being cared for, they can trust their physical and social environment, and can trust themselves in that environment. Parents as the primary caregivers are the ones who help infants to develop this trust which is necessary if infants are to continue to higher stages of emotional well-being. Without basic trust, basic mistrust develops and children never learn what it is to entrust themselves to others or to trust themselves.

In Stage Two—*Autonomy vs. Shame and Doubt*—children learn a healthy sense of personal autonomy and separateness from their parents and others. Yet this autonomy does not mean that they do not need others. They still need love, care, and nurture. Children at this stage, however, have discovered themselves as separate individuals—"I'm me!" is the answer given to the question "Who's Bobby?" Children learn to express themselves without being ashamed or in doubt about their acceptance by others in their family. They do not doubt their value or worth.

In Stage Three—*Initiative vs. Guilt*—children begin to plan and do things that are purposeful and active. Children learn to be active for themselves and initiate things themselves. Children eagerly learn from others, become involved in self-directed learning on their own, and work well with others. Children need to avoid feelings of guilt over what they are trying to do and of acting too aggressively with others.

In Stage Four—*Industry vs. Inferiority*—children learn to harness their feelings in order to learn in a structured environment. They are being taught that which their societies of school, home, and church believe are important to learn. Children in this stage learn that they must apply themselves in order to make progress as people. If they fail here, they will feel inferior and inadequate and they will not have the abilities to function in the real world. In this stage, children work together and alongside of each other, learning how to work cooperatively rather than as independent, autonomous individuals.

In Stage Five—*Identity vs. Role Confusion*—adolescents are able to develop a sound and continuing self-concept. Youth begin to answer the big questions of life: Who am I? Whose am I? Where am I going? And what will I be? It is not unusual for young people to decide for one reason or other that they will not try to answer these big questions of life. They are just going to live without having to think about serious issues. If youth are not successful in identifying themselves, they can end up with role confusion, the inability to know who they are, what they are about, and where they are going. Youth experiencing role confusion are totally confused about who they are and unable to really function effectively in their home, school, church, or outside societies.

Part of the sense of alienation from others and the disruptive behavior that many youth evidence toward parents and other perceived authorities seems to be caused by their desire to define themselves apart from their childhood supports and supporting characters—namely, parents and significant others in their lives. For adolescents to know what they are and who they are is a major accomplishment in these ten years of moving from childhood to adulthood. Part of the self-identity deals with their sexual self: they identify that they are male or female and begin to examine the various sex roles that are assigned to the two sexes. Today's society, where sex roles are changing, only adds more confusion to youth who are already confused and will be so for several years to come.

Affective Characteristics

Some certain general affective characteristics of children at different stages of their lives are examined as follows.

Infancy. What mother can forget the cry of her newborn infant—a cry that suggests from birth on that the infant can experience some sort of emotions. If an infant is restrained or a painful stimulus is given, for example an injection, the baby will cry and might even show anger. Interest, distress, disgust, happiness, surprise, fear, anger, and sadness—all of these basic emotions seem to be present in most infants within the first few months of age. It is not surprising to observe that children will respond to soft stroking and pleasant sounds in the first two weeks of their lives. By the fifth week of life, a mother's voice will produce a smile in an infant. And laughter appears at around the twelfth to sixteenth week. After a basic but rather rudimentary self-concept has begun, in which a child knows that he or she exists and can recognize that the face in the mirror is his or her own and not someone else looking at him or her, then the beginnings of the emotions of shame, guilt, envy, and pride will appear.

At about age six months children begin to show mutual affect, or some sort of empathy for others. They will cry when other children cry, they will look sad when an adult or other child makes a sad face at them, and they will be excited and joyful when someone acts this way toward them. Though children of this age do not appear to show signs of thinking, they do have an ability to feel the emotional tone and, it sometimes seems, the actual emotion of those around them. This suggests that busy working parents need to be careful what emotions they demonstrate while with their infants as well as when they are with their older children.

By the time children are two years old, they have developed strong likes and dislikes for food, people, certain toys, animals, and activities. Very simple interpersonal friendships develop in which children not only recognize another child their age but welcome that person into relationship with them.

Preschool. Preschoolers are sensitive to their emotional atmosphere. They reflect what is going on around them emotionally; calmness of atmosphere likely leads to a calmer child, and a hurried, frazzled atmosphere full of stress has its own affect on children. As we said before, many of the basic emotions of adults are felt by children, but they are not able to identify them nor are they able to talk about them by receiving any direct cognitive input from others. When parents are leaving for work and must drop off their preschoolers at a day-care center or at a baby-sitter, it would be wise for them to try to reduce the amount of stress that they are feeling. Otherwise, the preschoolers begin their day with the emotion of stress rather than relaxation.

Because children are sensitive to their emotional atmosphere, they are easily impressed by and receptive to the emotions which surround them. It is good to know that while they may pick up parents' stresses in the morning, children can also be redirected by a loving and cheerful caregiver after the parents leave. Of course, not having a stressful or other negative emotional atmosphere to begin with is even better. Why start a child's day out with a negative emotion? The same is true for the evening when picking up one's children from day care. There is no point in communicating to your children what a miserable day you had and how emotionally drained you are. A quick prayer to the Lord to lift your spirits for your children's sake is appropriate at this point. Ask Him for the joy of the Lord, rather than the depression of your day!

Preschoolers feel wonder and awe. Watch their eyes get big when they see something that they either like very much or that is a pleasant surprise to them. So many of their experiences are new, and each new positive experience is accepted excitedly. Preschoolers can also be fearful of the new and the unexpected, or of the loud noise that surprises them. Parents need to gently introduce new things to them, such as a new caregiving setting.

Preschoolers often like to cuddle. Remember that most of their learning comes from sensori-motor experiences. One of the most important concepts for them to learn is love. Love cannot be taught by words or definitions or pictures. Love is something that must be felt for preschoolers — felt by hugs, by kisses, and by being cuddled. One of the greatest things that parents can do at the end of their workday is to give their child a big hug and just hold their child in their arms for a minute or two, saying "Daddy and Mommy love you so much!" Then give them a big hug and kiss.

Physical expressions of love to children by their parents are irreplaceable actions that no one else can do for children. Only parents can show parental love and must take the opportunity to do so as often as possible. A time will come in later elementary years when boys especially will be less comfortable receiving that sort of expression. By the time children are in junior high (early adolescence) they will shun such expressions of love not only from parents but from everyone else as well. Somewhere around late junior high or high school age, they will begin to look for loving expressions from people of the opposite sex.

Preschoolers continue to develop empathy. When our daughter was about four-and-a-half, she asked for a camera for Christ-mas. Being the "insightful" parents that we were, we bought toy cameras for both our daughter and our two-and-a-half-year old son. We did not find out until later when Beth Ann was in high school that what she had actually wanted was a *real* camera, not a toy. But she did not want to hurt our feelings by not enjoying our gift to her. So she pretended to like her camera, even playing with it, all the while wishing that we had been truly been insightful parents who knew what she really meant! Talk about empathy! While this story is not the usual behavior of four-year-olds, it does demonstrate that even relatively younger children do feel what others feel and know how to function with them although they are not consistently so sensitive to others. Parents must be aware of this sensitivity and help their children to continue to develop it.

Early Elementary. Early elementary children have strong emo-tions; they laugh and cry and get angry, and they show all of these in full force. Often parents will express their own anger at such displays, especially at the negative emotions. Yet while parents need to teach proper expressions of anger and sadness, they should be thankful that their children do have these emo-tions and do express them. Affirm the emotions while still help-ing your children to express them in socially acceptable ways.

Strong emotions go along with the fact that early elementary children can be easily aroused emotionally. Fathers sometimes like to roughhouse with their children just before bedtime. How often a mother will say to her husband, *"You've* got them all wound up; *you* put them to bed!" Both fathers and mothers need to realize that strongly felt and shown emotions require parents to be sensitive to their children's easily aroused emo-tional states. But often in the early evening or on weekends there is still plenty of time remaining in the day to have a good romp and be filled with lots of emotional energy. Let your chil-dren know that they can shout and scream out without being censored. If adults and adolescents can yell and scream at ball games, why can't children do the same when they are excited about their "sports," whatever that "sport" might be?

As children grow older, they develop even more sensitivity to others and can express empathy. That is, they can express how others are feeling and can imagine how the other person might feel about a certain event.

This means that children from this age on can be helped to become more empathetic by having parents actually tell them to put themselves into the other person's place: "If you were that other person and this happened to you, how would you feel about this?" Then ask them why they would feel that way. Parents can also help by their own empathetic responses to their children. When their children are sad or mad or fearful or joyful, parents can express how they feel that same emotion and show how they indeed have the perspective of the children in mind accurately.

Late Elementary. Late elementary children would like to appear unemotional, in control, and not easily excited. They want to appear "cool," and not express their emotions, following the example of their perceptions of many adults. Yet they have very deep feelings and can be extremely sensitive to those around them. They often have fears that have stayed with them from their preschool or early elementary years.

How they learn to express emotions is rather crucial: If they have learned how to express their feelings in a healthy and acceptable manner, then these children can be encouraged to continue to do so. The model that the primary adults around them have set will help them to know how to do this. They will be ill-equipped to enter into their teenage years, if they have not developed healthy and socially acceptable means of expressing their emotions. Angry outbursts, gross impatience, selfishness, and such behavior by parents are not the way to help children control and express their emotions. Parents do need to show how they can be angry and not sin.

Adolescent Years. The teenage years often begin as an emotional roller coaster and eventually smooth out to be fairly adult-like by their early to mid-twenties. Often, adolescent emotions are intense, confused, and chaotic, showing extremes of emotions.

Youth have intense inner feelings and responses but lack the control that they had in their late elementary years. Little stimulus is needed to "set them off" into fits of laughter, ridicule, or sadness, especially during the first years of adolescence.

On the negative emotional side, youth show deep emotions of worry, self-pity, anxiety, anger, hostility, fear, superiority or inferiority, selfishness, pain, loneliness, insecurity, frustration, and closed-mindedness. It is not unusual to discover that some youth have a sense of alienation caused by disorganized, disruptive, or disintegrated families.

On the positive side, adolescents show pleasure, laughter, love, altruism, self-assuredness, and joy. They are seeking freedom, self-confidence, someone to love and to be loved by, acceptance, understanding, belonging, independence, interdependence, and stability and security in a world where everything seems to be changing—from their bodies to the political situations around them. Slowly, with many fits, starts, and regressions, they continue to move forward to achieve a sense of closeness with others who will accept them as they are. Undoubtedly, one of the most crucial affective developmental components is to achieve some sort of ego or self-identity.

Parents must have a huge amount of patience, understanding, forgiveness, and agapic love. Parents need to remember when they themselves were teenagers—something most of us have tried to forget. It is one of the most profitable experiences imaginable for parents to recall their adolescent years, the feelings and difficulties, and the strong desire for understanding, acceptance, and unconditional love—all of which too often were never received or not in sufficient quantity and quality.

Parents also need to give adolescent children opportunities to express their feelings. When a child comes home from school all bent out of shape by some perceived or actual insult or wrong, listen to the young person express his or her feelings, frustrations, etc. Help your adolescent children express how they hurt inside, and help that internal hurt to be talked through. Unfortunately, adolescent males especially have been given the idea that "real men don't cry," and thus they suppress their emotions. Giving expression of emotions in positive ways is healthy and far surpasses psychotherapy in adulthood.

Youth need unconditional, unfettered love from their parents. Studies have consistently shown that parents have the greatest impact on the values and outlook of their adolescent children. Parents are to this very day the single most influential power on their children, bar none!

Youth also need to be integrated into their families in ways appropriate for their new developmental achievements in physical, cognitive, social, moral, and spiritual development. Parents can do this by including them in "parental discussions" about major changes coming the family's way. This allows the young person to make significant and meaningful contributions to the family. Be sure to thank them when they have done so, and give them a direct voice in decisions that affect them—to the degree that you can follow those decisions. Show that the family needs the young persons in it, that these youth are not a bother or a pain but are loved, accepted, wanted, and needed as part of the family.

On more than one occasion during our own children's adolescent years we told them that there was nothing they could ever do to make us stop loving them. Our two children have expressed, both when they heard those words and from time to time since then, how important it was and is for them to know that our love is not conditional. We think that perhaps unconditional love, acceptance, and high regard for their personhoods were very crucial to their affective development.

CONCLUSION

Children are social and emotional beings. Emotions are the "spice" of life and social interactions are "food" on which the "spice" is sprinkled. From earliest infancy, children begin to show that they are social-emotional individuals. But so much of social and affective development hinges on parental involvement. Parents contribute very critically to these two areas.

Check up on your child/children's development and your observations.

Fill out the sheet individually. If you are married share your answers with your spouse.

Describe each of your children in the two developmental areas that follow. Then add what their development would suggest that they need from you as a parent. List at least six to eight characteristics in each developmental area and at least an equal number in the developmental needs column. (You may want to review each section of this chapter to see some of the major developmental changes that take place in children.) Feel free to add more from your prior knowledge and observations.

Social development characteristics	Developmental needs for parent(s) to supply

Affective development characteristics	Developmental needs for parent(s) to supply

Seven.
Leading Your Child
in Faith

Will our children have faith? Good moral values? These are most Christian parents' main and ultimate concerns. What can a busy, stretched working parent do to address these questions?

There is within each of us as human beings the innate drive to know God and to do what our conscience tells us is right. Yet we tell God that we would rather do it ourselves, be our own god and/or construct our own god in our image; we really do not want to know the God who has made us in His image. But this condition called sin is not the created condition. We as humans were made for God, and as Augustine said, "Our heart is restless until it rests in Thee."

MORAL DEVELOPMENT

Quite surprisingly, the foremost thinking on moral development came from one who did not profess any formal religion. Harvard researcher and writer, Lawrence Kohlberg.[1] Kohlberg's insights into moral development help our understanding of how children, adolescents, and adults develop from less to more mature persons in their moral thinking and actions.

Moral judgments and actions have been classified into three levels. A fourth level has been identified[2] from within a Christian perspective. Note the onset age of each level. Keep in mind that many adults do not move from Level One or Level Two throughout their entire lives. Each person develops at a different pace, and some stop at the earlier levels.

Level One—Focus on Consequences

Level One moral thinking and action is concerned with (1) the physical consequences that occur to a person and (2) what feels good when one does something. People decide if something is right or wrong either by determining whether or not the physical consequences are acceptable, or by how they feel about the results. If they get punished, then they will not do something. If they like what happened, then it is good. If they don't, then it must be bad.

Much of the marketplace morality in business, industry, and politics operates on this level of moral thinking and actions. An awful lot of bargains are concocted based on no one getting hurt and all feeling good and liking the results rather than on what is just and loving. Children and many adolescents think in similar ways. To be sure, children and youth do not have the sophisticated experiences and longer lifetimes of adults, but they do have the same moral thinking and actions that place them squarely on Level One.

Preschool children cannot make moral judgments nor are their actions intentionally moral or immoral. They do not have a moral capacity for making the distinctions between good and bad. Preschoolers can associate bad or good consequences with certain actions, and then begin to learn that those actions are good or bad. But in their minds it is not what they do but what happens to them as a result of their actions that makes something good or bad.

Parents obviously cannot wait until their children are six or seven or even older to begin to teach them about moral actions and moral judgments. But parents should not delude themselves into thinking that preschoolers, or even early to sometimes middle elementary children, have any idea that some things are wrong. Children need to be taught through punishment and rewards what are good and bad things. They will learn through experiences that certain of their behaviors and the inner thoughts which produce those behaviors receive punishments or rewards. Then children begin to realize that certain of their actions and thoughts have negative or positive consequences. They learn about moral actions and thinking, not from reasoning but from the physical consequences that occur to them.

Children—and youth and adults—who function on Level One need to know that their actions and thinking do have moral consequences for them. It is not wrong to think and act on Level One; it is simply not good to remain on this level for one's whole life.

Parents of children who are functioning on Level One should be aware that the primary way to influence their children's moral actions and thinking is to spell out the consequences for the children themselves. A parent could say, "If you do such and such, or if you continue to do it, then this is the negative thing that will happen to you." Or the parent could say, "Because of your actions, this is the punishment that you receive for doing a naughty or bad thing." In both cases, the punishment—either promised or actual—must fit the wrong done. The wrong must be a moral wrong and must be a part of a larger value system that the parents are trying to teach their children. To punish one's child because he or she was annoying you is hardly a moral issue as far as the child's behavior; it is a moral issue rather for the parent if he or she selfishly punishes a child for annoying the parent.

Parents should not tell their children that they are bad or naughty. Their actions and decisions are sometimes bad, but they themselves are not. Children do not have negative or bad value. We are all made in the image of God, and while that image has been soiled by Satan and our sin, God values us so much that He sent His only Son to die for us. God's action in sending Christ expresses just how valuable we really are to Him!

In order for a child to understand how to make correct moral choices, judgments, and actions, moral instruction must be received consistent with a larger framework of moral thinking, greater than the child's own. If parents do not function at a level beyond that of the child's, then the child will not likely become more mature in his or her moral thinking and actions. In fact, the child will become developmentally thwarted, and will never mature in recognizing that there are more adequate ways to think and act morally.

Parents can help a child on Level One by asking about the consequences of actions. Point out the negative or positive results of actions and ask the child why these things happened. Most children will say that good things happened because the person did something good, or conversely, that bad things happened because bad things were done. Generally, their observations about reality are correct. People go to jail because they are bad, not because they are good. People get tickets for speeding, not because they were obeying the speed limit. Children get punished because they do something morally wrong, not because they did something morally right. On the other hand, good things normally happen when we do morally correct things. People appreciate and like us, they give us rewards, they smile at us, they tell us that we have done a good job, they congratulate us, etc. And we feel good about all these things.

Children need to know that there are positive and negative consequences of their actions; they can predict which will happen based on their prior consistent experiences, especially with their parents. But parents must do more than be the punishers or rewarders of moral actions. They need to discuss with their children, even at Level One, ways of moral thinking, *why* certain actions are right or wrong. What matters is something deeper than just the consequences. What ultimately matters is justice and agape love. Good and bad are not determined ultimately by immediate consequences, nor even long-range consequences. Some things are wrong in and of themselves.

Busy working parents who are interested in helping their children learn right from wrong need first to help their children know that what they do has serious consequences for them. The children will learn early that if they do something morally wrong, they can expect to receive punishment or some consequences that they will not like. And they need to know that if they do what is morally right, then good things will happen to them. Could this lead to children looking for rewards and seeking to avoid punishments? Yes! This is the problem with Level One. Adults, youth, and children who are stuck on this first level cannot think or act beyond the idea of calculating the consequences. This is fine for a younger child who is morally immature. It is a sign of moral immaturity when this happens to an adult or mid-adolescent (ages fifteen to eighteen).

Level Two—Focus on Others
Persons on Level Two focus on what significant others think about them, or on what the law and other authorities say about their actions and thoughts. They are no longer primarily concerned with the immediate consequences of their actions. Children on Level Two are concerned with the outer influences of authorities who are important to them—parents, friends, older brothers and sisters, teachers, pastors, grandparents, special aunts and uncles—all become strong influences on these children. And the law, as embodied in the laws of the land, in our courts, and God's laws, is also very important on this level.

Normally, these children (starting at around age twelve to fourteen or older), as well as older youth and adults, have a very high regard for what some authorities outside of themselves think is morally correct. These outside authorities can be either people, a personal relationship with Jesus Christ, or the more abstract idea of laws and regulations of our society or of God. Persons on Level Two act morally correct because they are concerned with how some authority or authorities in their lives will look on their actions and thinking. Without rules and without authorities such as parents and friends in one's life, one would not know what is right or wrong.

God, who made the ultimate rules for the universe, is obeyed because He made good rules for humans. For older children and youth on this level, Scripture becomes very important in their moral decision-making and actions. So also is God as a friend. People on this level want to please God and to obey Him, not just because they want to avoid punishment or get rewards but because they love and respect Him. God is the most significant Person in their lives. He knows what is best for us all and made those rules, or moral laws to help people get along with each other.

Parents should keep in mind that their children, now of adolescent age, are responding to social clues and direct rules about what is morally right or wrong. Bring in input from those who are viewed by their children as significant outsiders. Thus well-liked relatives, friends, teachers, youth leaders, pastors, and ultimately God Himself, need to be brought to focus on issues of right and wrong.

In the final analysis for people on Level Two, something is morally correct or morally wrong because someone, Someone, or some law says it is so. It is to these sources of authority that parents may appeal, provided that the sources are respected by the children.

One of the tasks of parents is to assist their Level Two children in learning to think through the process of making moral judgments and actions. Take a few precious moments to discuss with your children what significant others think. It is important that children receive input from others' thinking about the morality and reasoning of certain behaviors. The intent of the heart and mind are often of equal—if not more—importance to God than the actual act itself. How one thinks is of vital importance to moral development.

This all may seem quite imposing: parents need to talk with their children not just about what is morally right but also about *why* a particular thought and action is morally correct. The parents' and other respected authorities' thoughts should be a part of the discussion. We as parents want our children to continue in their moral development, not be stuck at a lower level. We should assume that as one of our primary responsibilities and not depend on other people in our children's lives to help them in their moral decision-making. The issues are clearly joined: either parents take their responsibilities in hand or someone else will when it comes to raising our children.

Moral issues are constantly with us—discussing moral issues does not require parents to take special classes. Throughout each day a parent probably faces moral decisions and actions on his or her job. Newspapers, the evening news, MTV, and most TV programs and movies present us with dozens of moral issues. Parents need to recognize a moral issue when it arises naturally in their daily lives and then ask their Level One or Two children how they would go about solving the issue. The ensuing discussion will be the stimulus to help the children, as well as the parents, come to a clearer moral decision-making process and to a more nearly correct moral behavior.

Moral issues that are not clearly decided by appeal to a clear human or divine law are especially important to discuss. When something is morally ambiguous or presents a moral dilemma, it calls for us all to look at the whole moral question. We must examine other viewpoints, seek to determine the principle behind the moral laws we might cite, seek to understand the teachings of Scripture as applied to the particular moral issue, and look for ways to solve the ambiguity lovingly and justly.

By conducting such discussions around the dinner table or while chauffeuring children to an activity, parents can use informal times to help their children move from less to more mature in their moral judgments and behaviors.

Levels Three and Four
Levels Three and Four are not found in children nor, usually, even in high schoolers. These are quite mature levels and they demand both a longer life than that of a teenager, and many experiences to help temper and educate the individual's moral thinking and actions. We will only briefly sketch these two levels, since so few children under eighteen are at these levels. The hope is that parents will see the goals of moral development from this brief description and thus will understand that toward which their children and they themselves are moving.

Level Three is concerned with the idea of justice, that is, that people will be treated equally regardless of their race, creed, age, sex, nationality, socio-economic status, etc. From a Christian perspective God is viewed as One who is just, justifying those who believe regardless of their character or social, economic, or national standing. God is no respecter of persons. He treats us all according to His own justice and therefore according to what we deserve. God's invitation is to "whosoever will."

If Level Three—the justice level—is a mature level which only people with much experience and years under their belt can achieve, then it stands to reason that the fourth level, Agape, is even more mature and demands much more development. Agapic moral judgments and behaviors are rooted in God's agapic love for us, i.e., to act unselfishly to each other, to help meet needs, and even to self-sacrifice. Parents are hopefully moving toward and into these last two levels. They can, in some cases only hesitatingly, point to them because they are still well embedded in Level Two themselves. But at least they know what is ahead and can continue their own development and in turn can facilitate their children's future development when the time is right.

FAITH DEVELOPMENT

Faith development of our children has eternal significance. But it also is extremely important for daily living. Who or what we place our faith and trust in makes a difference in all aspects of our lives. As in so many of the previous developmental areas, faith development is divided into stages. We will look at the four stages which children and youth can achieve in the first eighteen to twenty-five years of their lives with the proper aid of parents and other significant teachers and experiences.

Faith development is concerned with what we believe is the ultimate Person or thing in our lives—that to which we totally give our minds and hearts. For some, their faith is in nothing; these are atheists, agnostics, or naturalists. To these people faith is belief in themselves, period. Nothing exists beyond this life for them and they believe and act accordingly. But for many people, there is a deep commitment to the knowledge of someone or something beyond themselves.

For the Christian, the ultimate One to whom we can give our hearts, minds, and souls is the God who is revealed in Scripture and ultimately in His Son Jesus Christ our Savior and Lord. People believe in something and/or someone or Someone; they all, in a word, have faith. The issue is not then will people — and for parents, will their children — have faith. The issue is: In what will our children entrust their lives, to whom and for what will they commit themselves for now and eternity?

Researcher and faith development author James Fowler[3] has described this human process called faith development in six stages, the first four of these stages covering early childhood to the late adolescent years. It should be noted that Stages Two through Four can also be found in many adults.

Stage One — My Family's Faith
Stage One is based on the indisputable observation that children's faith in their early years is virtually the same as their parents' faith. If a child is born into a Hindu family, the first four to seven years of his or her life will undoubtedly be filled with Hindu religious beliefs and practices. And if a stranger were to ask a child of a Hindu family if he or she were a Hindu, the child would undoubtedly say yes. This is true for children who are brought up in homes that are Jewish, Lutheran, Baptist, Presbyterian, Assemblies of God, Catholic, etc. The children in their first stage of faith development depend on the teaching of their family. They imitate their family's beliefs and practices. It is not unusual for Christian parents to find their children playing church or Sunday School with a child taking the role of the pastor or teacher and the other children taking church roles as well.

For such children, there is no real choice about the content of their simple faith. To most of them, this is not saving faith; it is imitative faith. They will go through the motions of what they are told to do. But they probably do not have direct experiences with the ultimate reality beyond those rituals and practices of their parents' faith.

However, it is not unusual for some young children, exposed to the Gospel at ages three to six, to respond to what they hear. They hear the Gospel because their parents are already Christian and explain to them the need for Christ to come into their

lives. But they respond to it as a result of the work of the Holy
Spirit, who convicts of sin and who regenerates a person and
transforms the child from a child of darkness into a child of
God. For both of us who are writing this book, we gave as much
of our lives as we knew about to Christ by the age of five. And
at ages four or five, both of our children, quite independently of
us, did the same. So, while children in Stage One reflect their
parents' faith, beliefs, and practices, they also can begin to internalize those beliefs and practices in their own simple and quite
immature, but nevertheless real, ways.

Parents should not be reticent to talk to their children about
giving their lives to Christ. Obviously, children under the age of
twelve or fourteen who cannot think abstractly (see chap. 4)
will not be able to internalize very much about God, sin, redemption, salvation, justification. But they can know that they
have made a very significant statement to the God whom they
have felt around them since the very early days of their con-
sciousness, and whom their parents worship and serve. Their
commitment is not a mature, well-reasoned one. It is a simple
trust in God, introduced to them by their parents. Yet, before
sin has taken its insidious hold on them, they have said yes to
the revelation of God's character and work for them to the
degree that they know how. They have become members of
God's family. Now, just as they need to be nurtured in their
physical development, they need to be nurtured in their faith
development. That faith development will continue along predictable stages.

Parents need to surround their preschoolers and early elementary children with experiences, books, TV, tapes, and church
contacts, especially ones that stress who God is. Parents who are
wise and effective in their parenting will talk about God in a
natural way as part of their daily life—in those "Teachable
Moments." They will read a Bible story to their children either
at one of the daily meals or at bedtime. They will pray at meals
and with their child at bedtime, encouraging their child to express his or her prayers to God as well. By doing these types of
things, parents communicate to their children that God is more
than a special person who is only important on Sunday at a

building called "church." Rather, He is so important that the parents talk about Him throughout the day and talk with Him often in the presence of their children. Children will begin to get the idea that God is not some great Person who occasionally drops in to say "hello." He is the One who is constantly with us and cares for us and sustains us throughout all the day and night.

This sort of parenting for faith development does not require anything of the parents other than a growing faith and reliance on God throughout their daily lives busy though they may be. Our children will be more mature in their own faith if parents have an integrated faith in Monday-through-Saturday living and not just Sunday-go-to-church living.

Stage Two—My Church's Faith

Children at Stage Two of faith development begin to understand their faith commitments in a broader context than that of their parents and their parents' faith. These children begin to see themselves as belonging to a larger group of believers of some local church or assembly. They realize that it is not only what their parents believe but also what their local church believes and teaches about God that matters. For children, and some adults who never leave this stage, their local church becomes the source of the content of their faith. Everything that they believe comes from their local church and its pastors and teachers. These adults are the ones who are in authority and who have truth to deliver to the children. The children accept it without really thinking about its meaning. Children in Stage Two are recipients of the faith teachings and faith behaviors of their parents and local church.

As in Stage One, a child at Stage Two is not in an improper stage. In order to eventually have a personally thought-through and owned faith, one must go through Stage Two. This is the way God works in people's lives: They get their input from people who are respected and who are more mature in their own faith.

Parents can help their children in Stage Two of faith development by exposing them to church ministries for children and to the worship services. Church ministries for and to children make sense to most parents and hardly need any more comment. Exposing them to the "adult worship service," however, often seems like cruel and unusual punishment, even if there is a "children's sermon." Rather than make children sit through an hour or more of adult level worship experience, an adult service can become somewhat meaningful to the child, if the parents provide the proper preparation for their children.

Parents can explain simply, on their children's level of understanding (see chap. 3), what will happen during the adult service and what it all means. They can explain the hymns, the liturgy, the Lord's Prayer, other prayers, why there is an offering, etc. Children are usually interested in "adult things" as long as they are not boring and unfathomable. Parents can help their children to understand and to achieve some measure of comprehension of what the adult service means. By doing this, parents aid their children in achieving a more mature state of faith development.

When children receive input from their local church they will find that the church and their parents believe the same things and support each other. This provides a broadening perspective for children that suggests that God is not some local deity encompassed only by their family. He is greater and wider and broader than just "me and Mommy and Daddy and brother and sister." God is the God of a lot of people at church too. And equally important, we all get together to sing, pray, and learn more about God. This God must be quite a Person!

Stage Three—My Denomination's Faith
Stage Three faith development has been called the "junior high" faith. A person believes what he or she is taught by their local church and by their denomination or others who are similar to their local church. For instance, children and youth—and a good many adults—recognize that they are evangelicals. Not only is their local church evangelical, but also there are a good number of other churches and denominations and organizations that are evangelical. So they identify with this larger group that represents in a broad fashion what the local body of believers

teaches, believes, and practices. Persons in Stage Three see themselves in a broader network of believers. They are Baptists or Presbyterians or Assembly of God or evangelicals, etc. They receive from this larger network the teachings and practices that help to make them more committed to Christ.

People in this stage have not really critically examined their faith. They are still relatively passive in accepting what is taught and in practicing what they are told to do. If they are told that good Christians share their faith with others, they will try to do so too—not because they are convinced that this is correct but because some respected authorities have said that this is right to do. Their commitments, therefore, are to a large part defined by direct input from others. This is as it should be. Children, usually about fourteen or older, still need some predigested information and directed experiences to help them have the raw materials with which to develop their own "owned" faith which comes at Stage Four.

Parents who are effective and wise will provide multiple exposures to people and ideas that come from beyond just their local congregation. Watch a Christian TV program, listen to a Christian radio station, or watch a Christian video with your children. Then discuss with them what was being said, to what degree they agree or disagree with it and why, how the program and/or person is similar or dissimilar to their local church and how to know the differences between the two. Parents need to take the time to talk with their children about the children's faith in relation to the faith of their parents, the local church's faith, and a broader group or groups' faith.

Stage Four—My Own Faith

Stage Four faith development is characterized by the taking of commitments and beliefs very seriously. For the first time in their lives people are able to think abstractly and thus are able to examine the teachings of their church and larger groups of influence. Persons in this stage no longer merely identify with authorities outside themselves for their faith beliefs and practices. Now they are thinking for themselves and examining what has been taught to them by respected authorities. These people develop their own understanding of the faith that has been delivered to them and which they have received over the years from their parents and other teachers.

Stage Four is the first time in a person's life when they can honestly say that they have accepted mentally what they have been believing all their lives. They have now begun to understand truth not just as a package of things to be believed because someone else has told them, but because they have examined it for themselves and found that it is true. They have received within themselves the witness of the Holy Spirit that makes them open to input from Scripture in a new way, which does not need to be constantly explained by respected authorities.

Paul wrote to Timothy, "Continue in what you have learned and have become convinced of, because you know those from whom you learned it, and how from infancy you have known the Holy Scriptures, which are able to make you wise for salvation through faith in Christ Jesus" (2 Tim. 3:14-15). Timothy was surely taught by his mother and grandmother, but he also had to become convinced for himself that what these significant others had been teaching him since infancy was indeed truth. A Stage Four person is one who has become convinced that what has been taught him or her over the years of childhood are indeed true teachings. In turn, this person can give his or her whole life unreservedly to Christ in a new and more mature way.

Faith development will occur in our children. They will put their trust in something, someone, or Someone. What we parents do will affect their eternal destiny as well as their life on this earth now. We can help them to go from the imitative faith of Stage One to owning their faith as truly their own. God has no grandchildren, only firstborn children: "For you have a new life. It was not passed on to you from your parents, for the life they gave you will fade away. This new one will last forever, for it comes from Christ, God's ever-living Message to men" (1 Peter 1:22, TLB).

CONCLUSION

We must pray that our children will *have* faith and will *make* good, moral decisions. As we have stated in this chapter, parents are the first and continue to be the primary ones who influence their children's moral and faith development. Of all the six developmental areas that we have briefly described in chapters 4, 5, and 6, moral and faith development are at the heart of being Christian parents. If we fail here, then the other developmental areas are wasted. If we succeed here we have helped our children to trust in God eternally and to look to Him as they act and make moral decisions.

Check up on your child/children's development and your observations.

Fill out this sheet individually. If you are married share your answers with your spouse.

Describe each of your children in the two developmental areas that follow. Then add what their development would suggest that they need from you as a parent. List at least six to eight characteristics in each developmental area and at least an equal number in the developmental needs column.

*Moral development
characteristics*

*Developmental needs
for parent(s) to
supply*

*Faith development
characteristics*

*Developmental needs
for parent(s) to
supply*

Part Three.
Daily Parenting

Eight.
Why Families?

Why Do We Have Children?

Have you ever stopped to think about it? Why DO we have children? We never really took the time to think about it but just expected to have children as the natural progression of life. And we're glad we did. The delights of a family are worth it!

Why do you have children? Couples often feel that a child will bring them closer together, will help them to focus on a common interest. Many men want a son to continue the family name—a Junior to replicate the father. Many mothers want to enjoy and to sometimes "live their life" through a daughter, often helping her do and be what they wanted to be. In our situation we discarded this idea midway through our daughter's first-grade year, when she did not exhibit the high proclivity toward music her parents expected. Her gravitation toward acting and drama, her independence (in that way she followed her parents!), her style of dress, and choice of colors fit a free-spirited child. Early on we encouraged her creativeness in these areas, rather than trying to make her into her mother's image.

Is there a negative side to having children? They *are* a lot of work and cost quite a bit to bring up and educate. They cause tensions and bring frustration; they sometimes disrupt marriages; they make demands on time and energy; and often only complicate life, particularly for the working couple and the single parent. The single parent experiences these frustrations, but sees great joy in "having" the child/children. It is not uncommon to hear "at least I have the children from this broken marriage."

In spite of the negatives, the positives—the joy and fulfillment of having children—far outweigh the frustrations. It is worth all the difficult times to have your child respond with an "I love you," or a special smile and playful tease that are integral to this God-given relationship.

The family is a unit of strength, a haven, a support. And with family comes love, encouragement, understanding, care, nurture, and respect. Sound ideal? Well, from this end looking back, we can almost proudly reflect on our twenty-seven years of being family and see how each of these elements has at different times been true. But the credit must be to God's graciousness and the example that has been set forth by our own parents and grandparents and their strong adherence to scriptural principles. To take time and read what the Bible has to say is an exercise in reviewing history, and our special responsibilities in God's family. The tenets of this chapter are true for any family, but for the busy, overworked, dual-career couple or single parent, the time and priority of dealing with these truths need a primary focus.

Generations of faith are mentioned over and over again in Scripture. In biblical times, a great deal of respect and honor was given to parents, grandparents, and great-grandparents. The Bible points out that God blessed those families that lived and talked about and passed down their faith from generation to generation.

In our society we barely even know who our great-grandparents were, so many families have been fractured and blended a number of times. Often the traditional stories carried down from generation to generation are long lost. In spite of this, God promises and continues to bless families who put their faith and trust in Him for generations to come. In our family the "faith of our ancestors" has been carried to us from generations past. However, one does not need to be from many generations of believers to be a part of God's family. You can begin this history now for future generations.

WHAT IS THE PURPOSE OF THE FAMILY?

Scripture teaches five basic principles about the family. First, the family is a creation of God. Second, children are a gift from God. Third, children are to be dedicated to the Lord. Fourth, parents are responsible to teach and lead their children in all matters. Fifth, the home is the place to facilitate, aid, help, teach—in a word, nurture!

Family Is God's Creation

First, Scripture paints a vivid picture of the family as created by God, blessed by Him and directed by His unfailing love and concern.

The concept of family began with God. Its outworkings in various societies find its source in the fact that Father God is the One who heads up the family. "For this reason I kneel before the Father, from whom His whole family in heaven and on earth derives its name" (Eph. 3:14-15). The model of family, as it is manifested in its best forms, is based on the heavenly pattern of the Trinity in which there is perfect harmony, and is governed by God. The "glue" holding the family together is twofold. First, it is part of God's plan and second, it is based on the covenant of marriage. God's covenants are always grounded in His unconditional love for humanity. At the very heart of marriage is the unconditional covenant of husband and wife to each other: "Till death do us part." This covenant of love is the basis for bringing children into the world and for helping them to grow up in all ways to be more and more like Christ. In a society wrought with divorce and marital stress, couples should focus on the commitment to each other and the concept of marriage, and work to deal with fissures and cracks in their relationship.

Family is no accident of society. It exists because God created it. He sustains the family along with all the rest of the universe. Human beings live in family units because we are created to live that way, just as we breathe oxygen. The family is part of the natural order and is dependent on God's decree that it exist. God's covenants are a model for the family to follow as we live and work with each other.

Children Are God's Gifts

Second, children are a gift from God. That's right. We some-times forget this. Verses throughout Scripture, beginning with Adam and Eve in Genesis 4:1, 25 and continuing throughout the Old Testament, indicate that children are not just the result of intercourse between husband and wife. But rather, God gives them to the couple. As a gift, children are to be gratefully and joyfully received. (See Gen. 17:16; 28:3; 29:32-35; 30:2-6, 17-24; 33:5; Ruth 4:12-14; 1 Sam. 1:17, 19-20; Job 1:21; Pss. 113:9; 127:3-5.)

Children are not given to be used for selfish reasons, though there are sufficient examples in Scripture to show that some parents do so. (For instance, Jacob's two wives Leah and Rachel used their children to battle it out with each other for Jacob's affection, and God intervened in the whole matter in Gen. 29:26–30:24.) The parents' responsibility is to help their gift— their child—to develop into maturity. The story of the Prophet Eli and his two sons (1 Sam. 2) portrays an example of what God did *not* want to happen with the gift of children.

Children Are God's

Third, children are to be dedicated to the Lord. The dedications of Samson (Jud. 13:5-7), Samuel (1 Sam. 1:21-28) and Jesus (Luke 2:22-24) are three examples of such in Scripture. Jesus' statement, "Let the little children come to Me and do not hinder them" (Luke 18:16) suggests the same thing. The Lord's decree to Moses in Exodus 13:2ff bears this out: the firstborn male, whether human or animal, belonged to God. Humans were redeemed back by offering a special price of silver (Num. 18:16).

Children belong to God. The basic idea is the same whether they are baptized or dedicated in one's church. Children are given as gifts to parents who are to act as stewards of these rich human treasures.

Parents Are Leaders and Teachers

Fourth, parents are responsible to teach and lead their children in all matters. Scripture addresses this responsibility numerous times — too many to note them all here. The role of parents in the teaching of their children is described in the classic text Deuteronomy 6:1-9. Parents provide the atmosphere in which children will be stimulated to ask questions about their faith. They are to be ready to give answers, and to talk about these things at bedtime, at meals, and throughout daily life. It is assumed that parents know God's mighty works and can communicate what God has done for them, what He continues to do for their children and will for their grandchildren, and so forth. It should be that the whole of family life is infused with God's care and love for His people, and that His people do not hesitate to talk about Him at any time. That is the parents' responsibility and privilege!

Parents Are Nurturers

Fifth, the home is the place to facilitate, aid, help, teach — in a word, NURTURE! A short list of what parents do is found in 1 Thessalonians 2:11-12: "For you know that we dealt with each of you as a father deals with his own children, encouraging, comforting and urging you to live lives worthy of God, who calls you into His kingdom and glory." Paul states that fathers — and we think this includes both mothers and fathers — do at least three things as they help nurture their children. Parents encourage, comfort, and urge their children to maturity in Christ, or in his words, "Live lives worthy of God, who calls you into His kingdom and glory."

Encourage. The three actions of parents that Paul mentions above — encourage, comfort, and urge — are all nurturing actions. The root idea of the word "to encourage" is *to come alongside of.*

Jesus uses this same word to describe the Holy Spirit as the
Paraclete, the Comforter (KJV), and the Counselor (NIV). (See
John 15:26; 16:7-15.) The Holy Spirit comes alongside of us and
counsels, gives encouragement, comforts, and helps us. Parents
stand in relationship to their children just as the Holy Spirit
does to us: We are to comfort, encourage, counsel, and assist
our children in their growth and development. Jesus states in
John 16:5-15 that the Holy Spirit has a major role to teach us;
parents have a major role to encourage their children to learn
not only spiritual things but all things that the parents can teach
their children.

Comfort. The second word that Paul uses in 1 Thessalonians is
comfort. This word has similar meaning to the idea of encourage. In fact, both words could legitimately be translated comfort
or encourage. It seems that Paul sees that parents have a major
role in encouraging and comforting their children. Why? Because learning is not always easy. We usually learn best when
things do not make sense to us and we are struggling for new
ideas and new ways to do something. Remember when you
learned a foreign language or some new mathematics or a phys-
ics formula? It took a lot of work to actually learn and not just
memorize a bunch of data. You were probably uncomfortable as
you struggled with the new ideas and expressions. Note that we
used the word *uncomfortable!* Part of the parent's job as a teacher is to help the uncomfortable child to feel comfortable in the
learning of new material and ideas.

Urge. The third word is to urge. The actual root meaning of this
verb is *to bear witness, to testify.* From this Greek word comes the
English word "martyr" as one who testifies to his or her faith
even through death. In the Thessalonian passage it carries the
idea of an emphatic demand or an urgent action. And so it is
that parents do urge their children to learn all sorts of things.
Note, however, that Paul states that he along with parents
should not just encourage, comfort, and urge their children to
learn generally, but also in the specific area of growing up in
Christ.

Every wise and effective parent echoes Paul's comments in 1 Thessalonians 2:19-20: "For what is our hope, our joy, or the crown in which we will glory in the presence of our Lord Jesus when He comes? Is it not you? Indeed, you are our glory and joy." There is no doubt about it—when our children grow up to be mature in Christ and in other areas of their development, as whole people, they become our glory and joy. If children are a blessing from God, when they mature they are indeed a joy and glory for us and to us.

As wise and effective parents view their children, they must feel like 1 Thessalonians 3:8-9: "For now we really live, since you are standing firm in the Lord. How can we thank God enough for you in return for all the joy we have in the presence of our God because of you?" If we as parents have truly been encouragers, comforters, and urgent teachers of our children, then we can really live when our children walk in Christ and stand firm in Him.

Our prayer for our children follows Paul's for the Thessalonians: "May the Lord make your love increase and overflow for each other and for everyone else, just as ours does for you. May He strengthen your hearts so that you will be blameless and holy in the presence of our God and Father when our Lord Jesus comes with all His holy ones" (1 Thes. 3:12-13).

WHAT IS THE PURPOSE OF THE HOME?

Home is a place for husband and wife to "be one flesh" not just sexually, but in heart and mind. It is where love without human parallel can be expressed through the little and big things of life. It is a place to nurture our children in the things of Christ, just as the Holy Spirit does for us. The home is a place for parents to teach, urge, encourage, and keep on comforting the learners, our children, as they learn new lessons about life.

The home is not a place for a "commanding general" or a ruthless dictator. Nowhere in the New Testament—and especially not in the texts that we have examined in 1 Thessalonians—is it suggested that parents (particularly fathers) are to rule like monarchs, making our children fear and jump to serve us. In fact, Paul says clearly in Ephesians 6:4: "Fathers [and mothers], do not exasperate your children; instead, bring them up in the training and instruction of the Lord." "Exasperate" is better translated, "Do not provoke your children to anger." That is, don't exasperate them to the degree that they are justly angry. Imagine that! Paul suggests that parents could, and do, provoke their children to anger! That is *not* the purpose of the home.

Rather, the home is the place and the family is the group of people among which parents bring up their children in the faith. Children are taught the Christian faith in words, ideas, and rituals. But even more so, children are taught the Christian faith by what they observe in the daily lives of their parents, older siblings, extended family, and friends. "Training" refers to the idea of nurturing or feeding. The parents' roles are to care for, nurture, feed, and do whatever else is necessary to raise well-developed, well-nourished, mature children.

Home and family together comprise the environment and major stimuli for growth and development. The parents' major responsibilities are to provide positive environments and stimuli. Love, acceptance, affirmation, expressed appreciation, and family traditions, rituals, and practices make the home function as God intends. First, take *love*. Love is the key to both the husband-wife relationship and the parent-children relationships. First Corinthians 13:4-8 reminds us:

Love is patient, love is kind. It does not envy, it does not boast, it is not proud. It is not rude, it is not self-seeking, it is not easily angered, it keeps no record of wrongs. Love does not delight in evil but rejoices with the truth. It always protects, always trusts, always hopes, always perseveres. Love never fails.

Applying these verses to the family, one can easily see how we can improve our families immediately. Take, for example, *patience*—How many Type A fathers have patience with their Type B children? How many harried mothers, trying to balance work, family, and home have patience with their children's slowness to do chores?

How many husbands stop and think before giving unkind, unsolicited suggestions on house management? How many mothers or fathers think about the words they say to their children when they first walk in the door from work?

How many parents envy another family who makes more money and has only one working parent? How many single parents envy the married parents, working or not?

How many parents boast about how great their children are, fathers thinking that their children take after their side of the family and mothers after theirs?

How many parents are proud about their accomplishments, how much money they make, the vacations they can take, the extras that they can afford because of two incomes?

Acceptance is the process of communicating both in words and deeds that the other members of your family are all right in your eyes—they do not have to do anything special to be accepted. They do not have to prove anything to you nor fit your standards. Your children do not have to be "A" students or stars on the ball team. They do not have to make it to the top in order for you to truly accept them. They are accepted just as they are, imperfections and all!

Affirmation is acceptance plus the placing of ultimate value on the others in our families. It means that we not only accept each other, but we affirm that God has made us. We are in His image and therefore worthy of His unmerited love, as well as the love of spouse to spouse, parent to child, child to parent, and sibling to sibling. We all have great value in God's sight and we communicate that we value each other greatly in the family. It may take a major catastrophe for some of us to realize that we need each other, but we do, and we should learn how to express that.

Appreciation is the process of affirming the other's personhood and value, and of telling that person just how much he or she means to you. Dating couples often use various verbal and non-verbal means to show their appreciation to each other. Newly married couples continue that for a short while. Firstborn infants receive this same affirmation. But soon "the flower fades" and the new affection becomes old. Love is still there; acceptance is still a part of our feelings for the other; affirmation occurs from time to time; but appreciation is seldom expressed. We often don't even manage a thank-you for a well-cooked meal, for the income that the other provides, or for the household chores that the children do more or less willingly.

Appreciation is needed and useful to continue giving to each other. Without appreciation, love seems like an abstraction or a vapor that hardly exists. Appreciation expressed is the concretizing of inner love for the other. Without expressing appreciation, our family relationships wither and become old and brittle. Too soon they fracture and we wonder why? What happened? We stopped saying, "Thank you," and, "I love you." And we stopped giving little tokens of love and appreciation such as a special fruit or candy that we know our spouse or children really likes; or little trinkets from one of our trips out of town.

Family traditions, rituals, and practices are the precedents that parents set for and with their children in their earliest days. Our family has numerous traditions, especially at Christmas and other holiday times. Since preschool days, our now-young-adult children would not allow us to even suggest that we should drop them. Some things are just too important not to repeat. Traditions, rituals, and practices can be predicted to happen at certain times in the year, on special and not-so-special occasions. In a world that seems to thrive on the new, it is good to have some times in the year when the expected will consistently happen. Traditions provide stability and security in a world that has neither. Our children, and we as adults, need both stability and security to keep us from always being off balance, trying to right ourselves, in this topsy-turvy world.

Family traditions vary. Some families have a red birthday plate that says, "You Are Special Today." This is placed at the birthday person's spot on the table for the whole day. Other families have a number of traditions that they maintain from generation to generation. Our family holds a precise Christmas morning tradition, and has done so for at least 27 years.

Love, acceptance, affirmation, appreciation, traditions, rituals, and family practices teach values. They help our children to formulate their own values built on their experiences with parents and with the entire family. As was said in chapter 7, parents teach moral and spiritual values not so much by their didactic sayings as by their actions and their words of love, acceptance, affirmation, appreciation, and traditions.

A MOMENT FOR REFLECTION AND MEDITATION

One of the most difficult things for a working parent to do is find time for a quiet moment for Scripture reading, reflection, meditation and prayer — either alone or with one's spouse. And yet it's *the* most important thing in life. We are created to glorify God and enjoy Him.

So seize the moment — and read the following Scriptures which will help you focus on the Lord, the giver of strength. He is the one who sustains and brings joy and peace — to Mom, Dad and the whole family.

God placed people in family settings, but our family units in the late twentieth/early twenty-first century are drastically different from those of biblical days. As you read over these selected passages, ask yourself or share with your spouse:

How does our family fit the biblical framework?
What thoughts, feelings, and behaviors need to change so that we can help our family to be Christian?
How can the biblical passage be relevant to me, here and now?

Read one section each day for seven days and relate the Scripture to your situation. We think God, by His Holy Spirit, will challenge and energize you as you read, think, meditate, and decide how to become more effective and wise parents. These Scripture portions are just a few of the many that could have been chosen. You may want to add others. In fact, use these seven sections below for a week and then add your own portions each day.

DAY ONE
Be Righteous
Proverbs 20:7. "The righteous man leads a blameless life; blessed are his children after him."

1. Why are righteousness and blamelessness joined? How does righteousness lead to blamelessness? Recall the saying that if you tell the truth (are righteous) you never have to remember what you said. How do all these ideas fit together?

2. What do you suppose is the connection with righteousness, blamelessness, and having one's children be blessed?

3. For how long does our righteousness live after us? See Matthew 13:43; Philippians 2:14-16.

DAY TWO
God Is Your Strength
Read Psalm 46 and respond to these questions:

1. How often is God available to strengthen us?

2. What can shake God or diminish His strength?

3. If God is our strength, then what do we need to fear?

4. What fears do you have that need to be given over to Him?

5. What picture is portrayed in verses 3 through 7? Do you get the feeling of peacefulness or storminess? How?

6. What do verses 8 through 11 add to your understanding of the strength of God in your life?

Philippians 4:13 says, "I can do everything through Him who gives me strength."

1. What is included in everything? Obviously, nothing is excluded and all things are included. But do you believe that parenting is included in "everything"?

2. What do you need strength for today, or tomorrow morning? What are some "everythings" in your life where you need to be empowered by God?

3. Ask Him for that strength. Believe He will give you what you need—not exactly how you think it should be given, but as He sees your need.

4. Now relax! Read and meditate on Philippians 4:6-7, noticing the peace *of* God and the peace *from* God that are mentioned in these two verses. Let God's peace be yours.

DAY THREE
The Joy of the Lord
Nehemiah 8:10. "For the joy of the Lord is your strength." You should read verses 1 through 12 to get the whole story behind this one part of verse 10. The people seemed to be fairly well convicted of their sins and were really, to use our terminology "all strung out." Do you ever feel that way about life? It need not necessarily be because of your sin, though that might be one cause of such a feeling. Often we feel frazzled and so tired we want to give up! Try focusing on this verse when you just *can't* keep going.

1. What is the joy of the Lord? Is it joy that comes from the Lord or is it joy that belongs to God? Or both?

2. How do we get this joy? Read Philippians 4:4-7. Notice the repeated command to rejoice in the Lord! Why do you think that Paul repeated this? Read Galatians 5:22. How does this verse help to answer how we get joy?

DAY FOUR
Support
Matthew 19:5. "A man will leave his father and mother and be united to his wife, and they two will become one flesh."

1. Why is it necessary for the husband to "leave his parents"? Why do you think Jesus, quoting Genesis 2:24, said "father and mother" and not just the generic "parents"? Why is Scripture so specific about whom to leave?

2. Should we understand this verse to mean that the wife also should leave her father and mother? It would seem so. In the days of Genesis, a family was patriarchal. A wife really had no choice but to leave her parents' house and go with her husband. That is not the case now. So it would seem that the principle behind this verse is twofold. First, both husband and wife leave their childhood homes. And second, they form a new unit—not an integral part of either of their old homes but a new home. Why? Have you "left father and mother"?

3. Read Genesis 2:18-25.

Notice that one part of creation was not good. What was that? Why was it not good?

What was God's answer to the incompleteness of Creation?

What did Adam need, not just want but actually need, that God's own presence did not fill?

What was Adam's response to God's new and final creation?
Reflect on the relationship that is referred to in verse 18: "I will make a helper suitable for him."
How does "becoming one flesh," the sexual union, point to the marriage relationship as one of support?

DAY FIVE
Love
Read 1 Corinthians 13.

1. As you come to the descriptions of love in verses 4 through 8, ask yourself if the love you feel inside you and express to your spouse and/or children is characterized by this aspect of love. For example, "Love is patient." How patient have you been lately with those in your family? Would they know that you loved them by your patience or would they more likely say that you did not have love-patience for and with them?

2. Go through each statement about love and ask yourself these same questions.

3. Do not stop with just answers to the questions. Decide what you will do about showing love consistently to your family. Ask God to help you to work on just one of these areas for several days. Then go on to another one.

DAY SIX
Nurture
Read Deuteronomy 6:1-9.

1. Who is responsible to teach your children—Sunday School teachers, pastors, Christian day school or elementary or secondary school teachers? You?

2. Why do you suppose that parents are given this responsibility?

3. To what degree have you given a major portion of your children's Christian nurture responsibility to others? How can you change this? What will you need to know? What changes in your priorities will you have to make in order to fulfill this command?

Read Psalm 78:1-7; 2 Timothy 3:14-15.

1. What are parents supposed to teach their children about God?

2. How many generations can be involved in the Christian nurture of our children?

3. Why are the Scriptures an important part of the content we teach our children about God?

DAY SEVEN
Encouragement
Read 1 Thessalonians 2:11-12; 5:11.

1. What does encouragement mean to you? When someone encourages you, what kinds of things does he or she do?

2. How do you feel when you need encouragement? How do you feel when you receive encouragement?

3. Why is it that parents, "fathers" in 1 Thessalonians 2:11, are expected to give encouragement to their children? Why is this so important to the children? Does it do anything for the parent to encourage their children? How does it change the parents when they focus on encouraging their children rather than criticizing them or driving them to further excel?

4. Are you an encourager of your children? How can you encourage them more?

5. If you are married, how good an encourager are you for your spouse? What could you do to encourage him or her more? If your spouse is encouraged by you, how might that affect you?

Nine.
Setting Priorities and Identifying Roles

PARENTING IS PARENTING ... no matter what your life-style may be — dual-career couple, single parent, or the one-working parent family. The same techniques, skills, love, time, quality of experience, and relationship are as true of the dual-career working parents and the single parent, as they are for the family where only the husband or wife works. It makes no difference.

Why then a book for working parents? We've already talked about it; there IS a difference — TIME! This is not to downplay the busy lives of the at-home mother or father. The nonemployed parent is very busy. But the use of one's time, as has previously been discussed, is at issue in most situations. And the way you spend your time not only affects your children but also your own self-esteem and self-worth. A look at yourself, your attitudes, priorities, and lifestyle might bring some very surprising discoveries to you and your spouse. These discoveries may be helpful in refocusing priorities and managing your time. Single parents should read this chapter realizing your ex-spouse probably does not factor into a look at roles or priorities. Accomplishing these many roles alone is commendable — but don't be afraid to say, "I can't do it all!"

Evaluate your situation by asking "How do I make decisions and react to stresses and pressures? What is important to me, the driving force that makes me tick?"

WHAT OTHERS THINK

Feeling confident to think and make decisions for oneself is important. Not that one should disregard helpful advice and input from many other sources. But thinking for oneself also gives your children a model which enables them to learn and develop as healthy human beings.

Are the decisions you make and the ways you react based on what others think of you? Do extended family pressures cause you to be and act a certain way? These factors often drive or motivate us to make certain decisions. Often, following the death of a parent or grandparent, a divorce or other dramatic life-change will occur. Until then, there is a strong sense of not wanting to hurt or disappoint the family member. The family love and respect ties can be very strong and one often holds on through a difficulty until that person is "gone" before making a major change, for good or bad. These changes can be in career, geographic location, church, parenting style, cultural choices, etc.

The other side of this potential problem is the fact that many working and single parents need their extended family to help support and nurture their children. This help occurs in the practical concerns of childcare, or in occasional times of decision-making or traumatic events. Even for nonworking parents, there is a need for that extra aid and input that a grandmother, aunt, sibling, or cousin can give during times of stress. In our early years as young parents, Carol's parents and sisters lived in close proximity to us. Her activities and needs as a minister's wife were similar to those of a working mother. To be close to family in those very busy days was most encouraging and an invaluable time of growth and insight.

IDENTIFY ROLES

The roles that family members take within the family structure are governed by a very basic principle found in Ephesians 5:21, "Submit to one another out of reverence for Christ." Paul continues, giving some ideas of how this mutual submission is to be worked out between spouses, parents, employees, and employers. The same basic material is covered in Colossians 3:1–4:1. In both passages, holy living is the basis for the roles that Christians have in this world. Paul gives the rules for how to conduct one's household, as well as the basis for those rules. In Ephesians 5:21, the basis is mutual submission. In Colossians 3, it is setting our hearts on things above and doing all in the name of the Lord Jesus (vv. 1 and 17).

After the basic principles are laid down, Paul gets to the specifics of how the household should be run and how people are to relate to each other. We must not forget in reading the specifics that the general principle is first—submit to one another. We as Christians are in Christ and we deal with each other within the family as we are in Christ—we are one in Him (Gal. 3:28). So we start not with roles but with the fact that before God, we are one in Christ. This means that spouses are one together and they together are one with their children. This oneness and mutual submission and holy living means that we are always responsible for and to the others in the family. This is why Paul can tell parents in both Ephesians and Colossians that they cannot exasperate and embitter their children (Eph. 6:4; Col. 3:21).

As we look at roles, we need to keep in mind that we are one in Christ and therefore servants of each other for Christ's sake. Just as He came to serve and not to be served (Mark 10:45), so we as spouses have a primary role to serve each other and our children. We serve our children as nurturers and providers. But we also serve each other as spouses when we lovingly care for each other. It has often been said that the best thing you could do for your children is to love your spouse.

Should the working parents abandon their search for excellence? No. God intends for us to serve Him with our best efforts and this means in every aspect of life. But it remains nearly impossible to do everything that needs to be done in all areas of life and be at one's best. No vitamin will help you achieve this goal! A look at the roles that you must fulfill might be a first step in considering what you think your life should look like.

Sometimes roles can get confusing, and tensions can build up when roles and tasks overlap and are not clear-cut. Carol's favorite example of changing roles is the time she went to the spice cabinet, only to find everything in a different place. John, in the role of "cook," had decided to do some rearranging. Carol's first thought was, "Who is he to take over my kitchen?" She had to stop and realize that if she were to share the kitchen responsibilities (she gladly did so!), she must allow John the right to rearrange the spice cabinet if he liked. She should be thankful that he wanted to help!

Roles are constantly shifting, as times in life change with age, situation, personal need, etc. (As of the writing of this book, once again John has become the main chef.) Some of the roles you might be fulfilling are as follows:

Provider
The role of providing housing, food, clothing, and other necessities of life can be very confusing and unclear, particularly when both husband and wife are providers. How do you see yourself? If you're a working wife (particularly if you did not plan to work) you may feel resentment at having to be in this role. If you are supplementing the family income, you may feel less valued because you are working very hard and yet are not "providing," but "merely" supplementing. Or, you may be working for a specific goal: to pay for children's education (present and future), car payments, mortgage, etc.

If you're the husband, you may feel "taken for granted" and never appreciated. Or perhaps you may feel looked on with disdain for *not* being able to make enough to cover all of the bills. In our survey, one husband said that his wife does not like his profession and she works for money to take care of her own needs as well as to supplement the family income. As a result, the husband's self-worth suffers greatly.

With the growing number of remarried couples, often the husband is the provider, at least partially, for two sets of families, and there is undue stress for such couples. There is no doubt that this stress will affect parenting; the children will feel the effects of this unless the problem is dealt with.

Understanding why you're working, and understanding what your spouse expects of you may help you to avoid resentment that might build up over the years. When we moved to Southern California, we thought that Carol would only need to work for a year. But in the Southern California economy of the seventies and eighties, that never happened and it stretched into over ten years of full-time employment. Once she was comfortable with that fact, life was easier to handle. She is glad now that she's worked. She feels that she's a much better person as a result and has grown and had experiences that are irreplaceable.

As in all areas of the husband-wife relationship, it is very important to say "thank you for working" to each other and to show appreciation and affirmation, even in little ways. Our survey showed that affirmation from one's spouse and children was almost nonexistent. (Several received affirmation from their colleagues at work.) An ounce of love—a card, a note, or a kiss and "I love you and appreciate all you do" goes a very long way. It will be great for your children to see and hear you express this, for they will face the same, if not more difficult, societal tugs—they need to have the model that shows love and thanks to each other for the basic provisions of life.

Nurturer

The nurturing role is one that helps others to learn, grow, and develop into the persons that God wants them to be. One who nurtures teaches, so that a person learns, not just memorizes. The nurturer supplies the food for body, mind, spirit, and soul, in order that within a Christian family context the children continue to grow up in all ways to be more and more like Christ.

Nurturing carries with it the idea of the farmer who prepares the soil, plants good seed, and then cultivates the growing plant by giving it the necessary nutrients (or nurturing). The farmer knows that if he plants corn, corn will grow if he uses the proper nurturing that corn requires. So it is with children. Parents need to know that they are nurturing children, not a dog or cat or some wild animal. Parents help their children grow by providing the right kinds of food for their digestive systems, both literally and figuratively speaking. We would never give a piece of steak to a one-month-old infant because we know that the child's digestive system is not ready for solid food. So it is with all the other areas of human development.

Throughout the nurturing of our children, parents are continually encouraging, comforting, and urging their children's development from less to more mature. Parents teach constantly and incessantly through all the conscious and unconscious communications of values, ideas, and behaviors that they demonstrate while hardly even thinking.

Who is the nurturer in your family? Parents are. Along with providing, this is their primary role.

Listener

One who listens is one who is most wise. Too often parents do not listen to each other and even less to their children. The wisest parent asks lots of questions like "Why?" and "Why not?" "How come?" and "Why do you think that way?" He or she then listens to the replies—even the youngest child is able to verbalize his or her simple thoughts. Most of us were taught that parents do the talking and children the listening. But the wise and effective parent does a lot of listening to what is going on in their children's minds and hearts, and also interacts with those thoughts and feelings.

Sometimes the most effective parenting is done by listening to one's child after school or after supper when the child needs to "unload" the day's events and get some perspective on the day. In our family, Carol spent hours listening to our children, trying to make sense out of some of the typical turmoils of childhood and adolescent experiences.

Who is the listener in your family? Either parent can be and should be at one time or other.

Helper

A helper is one who takes care of the practical details of family life. Practical and necessary details include grocery shopping, running errands for the household like getting a loaf of bread or some milk on the way home from work, typing a paper for one of the children, helping with a school project like a bug collection for biology or a show-and-tell presentation, and so forth! All of these are details that someone must do. If done with a loving attitude, these can make for successful parenting and encouraging of the child's development.

Helpers seldom receive rewards immediately. Parents in particular need to be aware that helping their children will often go unrewarded for many years unless the children have learned how to be grateful and to express it to parents and others in their lives. Helpers help, not for rewards but because they want to and because they love their children. There is no compulsion involved with true helping. It is done freely. In one sense, helping is its own reward. Being thanked either immediately or a number of years later is "icing on the cake."

Both parents in the dual working family need to be helpers. In a single working parent family, the one parent must be a helper.

Schedule Setter and Keeper

This role is that of social director for the family. Someone must be in charge of the family calendar that hangs amidst the other "stuff" on the refrigerator door. The calendar keeper/scheduler is responsible to collect information about everyone's whereabouts for the upcoming months, write it down on the calendar and then maintain that calendar. The scheduler needs to know what is happening and when: PTA, children's school and church activities, either or both spouses' out-of-town trips, out-of-town friends' and relatives' visits, half-day and full-day school vacations, summer vacation, fall registration, sports, music and drama practices and performances, promotions in Sunday School, the holiday programs at church and school, etc.

Writing things on the calendar, however, is not an end in itself. The schedule keeper is the one who must maintain seemingly eternal vigilance on the activities of the days of the week.

How often a child forgot to ask mom to have those cookies baked for school until thirty minutes before leaving for school. We can almost count on the children remembering commitments when it is too late to keep them. So one of the parents needs to be in charge, not only of calendaring events and commitments, but also of keeping up with and asking for information.

The calendar/schedule keeper needs to plan social occasions for the family and for the spouses by themselves, and the times for family vacations. Obviously this person does not make the decisions about when, where, with whom, and for how long vacation plans will occur. But this person does need to raise the questions with the other spouse and with children who are old enough to enter into the family decision-making for such events.

Who is the calendar/schedule setter and keeper in your family?

Chauffeur
This is the person who drives children and picks them up and drives children and picks them up, etc., etc., etc. Oh, yes, and stops and picks up their friends and drops off their friends on the way back. The good news about being the family chauffeur is that it does not take a chauffeur's license!

Even better news is that you get to ride in a confined steel cage with your children for at least a few minutes (or much longer) and listen to them talk with their friends. They may even allow you to get involved in their conversation, but don't count on it. Regardless of how much you enter into your passengers' discussions, you will learn a lot about what they are thinking and experiencing, and all the sorts of things that you wished you could find out but were not quite sure how to bring up. Chauffeuring can give a parent a whole list of topics to talk about with the children when you arrive home. So instead of grudgingly driving the children around, look forward to it as an inexpensive means to learn what your children and their friends are talking about.

Who is the chauffeur in your family?

Liaison
A liaison is one who is a go-between, in this case, between one's children and the rest of the world in which both parents and

children live. Children and parents have relationships with people in the neighborhood, school, PTA, various church agencies such as Sunday School, children's choir, youth group, parents of children's friends, and friends of your children. The liaison makes arrangements with all of these different people, keeping in mind the calendar/schedule keeper and the chauffeur. It is often wise if the liaison is also the calendar/schedule keeper. She or he will quickly know what dates and times are available and who will be able to drive or have the house open for children's friends to come over, etc.

Who is the liaison in your family?

Correspondent

This person is responsible to keep the cards and letters going to friends and relatives. If your family is like millions of other American families, you have moved quite a distance from your former home at least once. You have friends and relatives who are not close enough to visit. Someone has to be responsible to send birthday and anniversary cards to relatives, especially to your children's grandparents. But your siblings and friends need to hear from you periodically—not only on special occasions. Friends and family need to know that you and your family have not ceased to exist nor stopped loving them. Someone needs to decide what sort of Christmas greetings you will send and get them out to friends and relatives.

One thing is certain, someone in the family must be responsible to communicate with your friends and relatives on both sides of the family. If no one is responsible, then no one will do it.

Who in your family is the communicator with close friends and family members?

Financial Overseer

This is the budget maker and bill payer. This person develops the family budget along with the other spouse, pays the monthly bills, keeps financial records in some semblance of order, figures out the income tax forms each year, pays insurance premiums, makes investments, and opens and closes accounts.

Not all of these financial actions can or should be done solo.

Investments and opening and closing accounts need to be a joint venture for dual working couples. A single parent would be wise to talk over financial strategy and decisions with someone else before making any financial commitments.

The financial overseer needs to keep the budget up to date. It is this person's responsibility to determine how much non-budget monies can be spent. This person will, after a few months, have a good feel for how the monthly bills come and how best to pay them. The financial overseer is the one who keeps the family honest about its expenditures. This person balances the checkbook each month and files the paid bills where both spouses and even older children can find them if need be. But no matter who handles this role, both spouses should be knowledgeable of their finances, and be able to step in, in case of an emergency or illness.

A word of advice on the subject of finances and planning: Be certain your estate is in order, your will, family trust, insurance, guardian for your children (in case of death or other disaster, etc.). Even the very smallest and simplest estate should be properly and legally cared for. We put this off, because we were always too busy working! You don't plan for an emergency—but it does happen, and we have known of children and a remaining spouse who have suffered because these matters were overlooked. It will take work—we found that one of us had to take this on as a project, or it would not have been accomplished.

This is a most important job for the family. Who is your financial overseer?

Social Director
This is the person who is responsible for determining who will be invited to social events at your house and how often. This person also makes the primary suggestions for either the whole family and/or just the parents to go somewhere for a social time.

It makes sense that the person who keeps the calendar and does the liaison work for the family should also be social director. But this is not a one-person task in a dual working parent family. Both spouses and older children can and should be involved in the decisions about social events for the family or for the spouses. We are not suggesting that children should tell the parents to go away for a weekend. But more than one parent has stated that their children have recognized their parents need to take a break and have some fun just by themselves. When your children are old enough to tell you this, listen to them and heed their advice. Set a date and go!

Who is the social director for your family?

Cook

Many readers will almost automatically say, of course, cooking is the wife's job. But this is simply not the case anymore. Many men have learned to cook either by their own will or for "survival." Depending on their age, children can be taught the appropriate steps to make simple meals or parts of meals. In many dual working households, cooking chores are shared depending on who is home first and which night. Some men find great satisfaction in cooking a complete meal. It gives them creative control over something after being controlled by bosses, time clocks, and deadlines all day.

Whoever does the cooking also needs to help make the grocery shopping list. If more than one person cooks, then all involved need to keep the shopping list up to date. There is nothing more frustrating than to begin to cook something and then find out that there is no more sugar or salt in the house!

Who is, or are, the cook(s) in your family?

Household Overseer

This person is in charge of the house, yard, garden, garage, car, and whatever else there is to be cleaned up and straightened. Obviously, this is a lot to do and one person often shares these tasks. They are lumped together here in order to show the large amount of work that it takes to keep a household and its family in some decent cleanliness and orderliness. Yards do not have to be spotless, but someone has to mow the lawn, rake leaves, shovel snow, sweep the sidewalks. Someone needs to do the laundry and put away clothes and linens. Someone must change sheets and towels. Someone must clean out the car. Someone must decide when a room or the whole house needs to be painted or redecorated. And someone must take out the garbage.

Many dual working parents split these household tasks between spouses and children. Older children can be taught to do their own laundry. Husbands often are the yard men of the family, with help from their children. Often a wife will suggest plantings that the husband and children will carry out.

The issue here, then, is which of the household tasks will each person in the household do? Who is responsible for what regarding the upkeep of the household in your family? And who will oversee all of this work?

Medic
This person is the one primarily responsible for the health of the children, taking them for their immunization shots, school physicals, and checkups. This is the person who gets up in the middle of the night with a sick child, and who keeps up-to-date medical records for each child.

Who is the medic in your family?

As we have reflected on the many parental roles, we have neither done justice to each description in this list nor have we been exhaustive with the many roles that parents fulfill in their parenting. The list could certainly go on. Add your own and describe them for yourself and for the others in your family. You will probably find some roles taken for granted: "Mom will always do that." But why?

If mother is a provider, then she should be treated like any other provider who has an equal part in the family operations. She should not be the one who works full-time outside the home and full-time in the home. Nor should fathers be subjected to the same sort of expectations. Nor should the children be expected to do all the housework because their parents work. There is a mutuality within a family that should and can be achieved. To be sure, when the children are infants and toddlers, the parents do it all. But as children begin to grow up, they must be taught to be responsible human beings.

SETTING PRIORITIES
"If you want to get something done, give the job to a busy person." That statement makes the working parent cringe. The

working parent cannot add one more thing to a schedule that already consists of more to do than can be accomplished. It really comes down to this: what is most important for the working parent? What really matters the most? What are my priorities? How can I manage to accomplish those things that truly do matter the most? The following section offers some ideas to help spouses, as well as the single parent, look at life and what is most important.

For Spouses
Talk to each other. Many women, and some men, want to take a segment of time, sit down with their spouse, and talk about life. They want to read Scripture and pray together. They function best when they can talk things out and be self-revealing.

Many spouses, however, do not function this way. They don't have the time and patience to sit and talk about life. More practically, they seem to organize their own time to fit the roles that they have already accepted in this dual working relationship.

The following questions might be helpful in your discussion: How do you make decisions? How do you react to stresses and pressures? What is the driving force that makes you tick? Look at these questions in light of the following: school, friends, sports, music, extracurricular activities, income, child's future education, friends, church, spiritual focus.

As with anything in marriage, if husband and wife are not agreed as to what is most important, then over time feelings and frustrations will build up and trouble comes. It is crucial for the working couple to get away from house and children—and any other distractions—and spend several hours together talking about the working/parenting/housekeeping responsibilities and their feelings about them. It is best to come to an agreement as to what priorities they each have, individually, and then as a couple. Many arguments, misunderstandings, and difficulties would be avoided by using this time for understanding each other and listening to the concerns and frustrations that each might have. Conflict, and even divorce, might be averted if this time together could be taken. It would be good to have such times regularly, at least twice a year, as a means of checking up.

It would be ideal to make this a romantic overnight "get-away" if possible, and include a special time for just being together, along with the time to set priorities. When our children were preschoolers, we (as a number of other couples do regularly) would take at least one night away and go to a nearby hotel for a day or two. Even though these times were mostly to get a break from busy schedules and be away from the telephone, we came back enthused for the work at hand and much closer as a couple—ready to take on the world.

During Carol's first year of full-time employment, or our dual-career employment, we did not have the time—or make the time—to just sit and talk about our lives and schedules. Yet Carol needed to sort through what she was doing and why. If we had been able to talk in depth then, misunderstanding and frustration could have been avoided.

Write It Down

The priorities and plans that a couple (or a single parent) makes should be put in writing, even if only in note form, so that there will be a reminder for the future. Each summer we talk and react to what is happening in our lives. Not having taken notes during the working years, we found that it was hard to recollect clearly some of the decisions we made, particularly as time passed.

How do you set your priorities? Start by writing out what you *really* value in life, and what you want to do with your life. List these things in order, ranking the most important number one. (See the end of this chapter for some suggestions.) It is crucial to have some idea of what you'd really like to do if you had the time and money. With this list, you can see very quickly what your priority in life is, and can keep that in mind as you look at the reality of your situation.

After you have gone through this exercise, sit down and write out the number of hours you spend each day and each week on various activities: sleeping, eating, preparing meals, talking on the telephone, carpooling, chauffeuring, working, parenting, shopping, watching television, etc. When Carol first went through this exercise, she was appalled at the way she spent time. What she wanted and valued most in life was almost nonexistent!

What Do You Value?

Many young married couples are returning or want to return to the values and lifestyle of the 1950s, when family was more traditional, Mom stayed home with the kids and Dad was the breadwinner. Yet it is virtually impossible in some parts of the country to think about living that way. In order to pay the bills, not only must the father often work at a job where he feels unfulfilled, but the mother must go to work as well.

To balance the reality of the situation, how do you maintain your existing values while finding ways of compromise? At this point, prioritizing your life becomes the critical exercise which will help achieve these values.

When prioritizing has been accomplished, what do you do with the results? How can you then take the data and make it practical, in order to have the values and ideals fit with the priorities? How can you take your hectic schedule and fit it in with what you really want to do? For some, it may mean a change in job and location. For others, it may mean a difference in attitude or lifestyle.

Listen and Love

Communication between husband and wife is most critical when both are busy and stressed. Being willing to listen and show love, as well as trying to blend one's personal desires with your spouse's, can make a relationship deeper and more enduring. So often the opposite is true and spouses end up judging and criticizing each other.

Spend time in Scripture reading and prayer together on a regular basis — even for five minutes. It may be awkward — many couples are not in the habit of doing this and if they do it is often perfunctory. Much love and sensitivity to each other's needs must be present in such a special time.

So, after you work through the exercises at the end of this chapter, look at what's important to you, prioritize your life, and don't sit there with lots of guilt and frustration. There's just no way you can get everything done; the time and priorities won't match up! But the important things will get done, if you keep focused and diligent. God's timing is always right, even in the smallest details of life. And a life committed *daily* to Him is life's number one priority.

A Footnote on Priorities

Have you ever heard the old expression, "Life is too short"? You could end up at mid-life with grown children, having missed all of the special time with your family. Time goes by too quickly— we and our children both grew older too fast!

As we mentioned earlier in the book, our family had an unexpected priority check one September morning a few years ago. Carol was awakened by John's saying, "Carol, I think I'm having a heart attack! Dial 911!" which she quickly did. God graciously provided a houseguest who knew CPR, the calm and quick thinking of our 22-year-old son who helped direct things, and the fast arrival of paramedics (who administered two defibrillations and got the heart beating properly again). John became a statistic, one of the less than 5 percent of those who live through such an incident. But the event brought us to some basic conclusions about life—what our priorities were and are. It helped us to realize how important we are to each other. And yet we had been so busy with work and living (we say, "existing") that at times we had forgotten just what was important to us. Even after that event, we still tend to get busy with life and forget the important things.

LIFE'S NUMBER ONE PRIORITY

"Man's chief end is to glorify God and enjoy him forever" (The Westminster Shorter Catechism). This is a good benchmark for refocusing on life and its true meaning.

Identifying Role Expectations

What do you expect from your wife?

What do you expect from your husband?

Are you meeting these expectations? Are they important and worth changing? How can you change?

How Much Time Do You Spend Each Week on the Following (hours and minutes)?

Cooking _____

Cleaning _____

Grocery Shopping _____

Clothes, Misc. Shopping _____

Watching TV _____

Personal Grooming, etc. _____

Chauffeuring the Kids _____

School Activities _____

Attending Church Service, Activities,
    and Committees _____

Hobbies _____

Reading _____

With Spouse _____

Family Outings _____

Social Life with Other Adults _____

Household Repairs and
    Maintenance _____

Gardening _____

Commuting _____

Work _____

Personal Devotions _____

Reading and Playing with
    Children _____

Business Travel _____

Community Volunteering
    (Committees, etc.) _____

Telephone _____

Sports Events _____

Homework with Children _____

Sleeping _____

Other _____

Other _____

Total your time and see where it is spent. Is this your list of priorities? What can you change?

Ten.
Taking Time

It's worth the extra time for the working parent to expose your children to a wide variety of experiences. Here are some we share from our family album.

SNAPSHOTS

Many little things may not seem like much to an adult. An afternoon excursion or the rereading of a favorite book may be an enjoyable quality time, and that's all, to the parent. But to your impressionable child, these types of events could have life-long impact. A trip to an aquarium at age three could spark a later career as a marine biologist. One visit to a convalescent home could instill a permanent heart of compassion for the elderly. You never know what small experience or exposure may make a difference in your child's development, interests, and personality.

A trip with our children to the Chicago Museum of Natural History and a look at the mummies set off in our four-year-old daughter a lifetime of interest and experiences in archeology, and a desire to share that with children through her writing. In fact, the influences of childhood—both small and large—have helped to shape both of our children into the adults they are today.

From the museum trips, the art lessons, exposure to all kinds of art, and the easel that John made comes a love for, a growing appreciation of, and an understanding of art of all kinds.

From the Boston Symphony's children's concerts, the annual performance of the "Nutcracker Suite," the playing of all kinds of music in the home—from classical to country, and the devoted attendance of the Monday afternoon band practices of the Michigan State University band, comes a love for and appreciation of a variety of music.

From the trips to the wildlife refuge, the classes at the Charlotte Children's Nature Museum, the backyard bird feeders, bird books, and trusty binoculars, the hamster that got away, and even the ant farm, comes an avid interest in the creatures of the world.

From the camping trips, with tent and shovel, roughing it in out-of-the-way spots, comes a love for the out-of-doors, the quiet places, and a resourcefulness of the true camper.

From the days and hours of reaching out to others in hospitality, and support to many in need, comes an understanding of sacrificial giving and mission.

From the hours of reading aloud comes a love for reading—aloud or alone.

From the backyard "pickle" games, sled rides in the woods, and driveway basketball comes a love for sports and activity of all kinds.

From encouraging the sense of adventure to try new and different things—notably escargot and alligator meat, for example—and getting to know people of other cultures and their customs, comes a love for the unique.

From the love for and time spent with extended family, comes a love and appreciation for family.

From the endless creative projects, the finger painting, fixing up a dollhouse, and making Christmas ornaments, comes a high sense of creativity and fun.

From the many, many childhood plays and "productions," and trips to the Children's Theater, comes a love for drama and acting.

From the hours spent playing Monopoly, Stratego, Scrabble, and Risk and seemingly dozens of other games comes the love for interaction with others in conversation and games.

From the hours of talking, sharing, and question-asking comes an ability to think for oneself and a sense of self-worth and independence.

From observing and taking part in ministry—from time spent with youth groups (when they were just young children) to caring for the needs of refugees—comes a heart of compassion, a giving spirit, and a desire for servanthood.

From the hours spent reading *The Narnia Chronicles* (over and over again!), many Bible story and Christian books, the breakfast table "Scripture Promises" box, and prayer requests, *The Savage, My Kinsman* by Elisabeth Elliot (and other such books) come hearts tender to Scripture and God's leading, a desire to dig for deeper meanings, and the will to be authentic Christians in all they do.

All of these things, experienced by children at their levels of development, have an untold effect on both their minds and their hearts. Some of these experiences require very little time from parents—a half-hour to read a book to a child. Others require planning and half a day or more—a trip to a museum or a play. But whenever we do these *with* and for our children, we do so with the sure knowledge that we are helping to nurture them like the young, beautiful, and priceless "plants" that they are. May God help us as parents to be wise and effective nurturers.

As you continue in this chapter, we've included some ideas to encourage resourcefulness (important for the working parents' attention), a potpourri of practical parenting ideas and activities, and some ideas for practical parents and their relationships and needs.

PRACTICAL PARENTING

Resourcefulness

One of the most important lessons that children of working parents learn usually earlier than other children, is that of resourcefulness. What exactly does this mean? Webster's Ninth Collegiate Dictionary defines resourcefulness, "an ability to meet and handle a situation; being capable of devising ways and means."

How do parents teach resourcefulness? By exhibiting love and understanding of the child's needs and by treating the child as an individual who is competent to think, feel, make decisions, and operate effectively at their level of development. We are convinced that by the time a child is eight or nine years old, the major part of their habits and thinking processes are already set.

At an early age a child can draw on their inner resources and life experiences and be very capable of fixing their own lunch or doing their own laundry. Our son began doing his own wash at age eleven — it was impossible for his working parents to keep up with his sports uniforms and many changes of clothes! By age five or six, he (and his sister) both fixed their own sandwiches, which also contributed to their need to be resourceful and independent. When David was about age seven, we left the children at home while we took a quick run to the airport for John's early Saturday morning flight. They were making their own breakfast toast, and a plastic bag which had been left on top of the toaster caught fire and flamed. While our nine-year-old daughter waited by the telephone to call the fire department (just in case!), our son got the fire extinguisher and put out the fire. Frequently there are stories on television of young children dialing 911 and helping those people in dramatic difficulties. We are convinced that children, even at very young ages, are quite capable of thinking and making decisions, and those who are in hard-working or single parent families usually, of necessity, are often even more so.

In our home we were careful not to make little slaves out of our children, to put all of the housework and dirty work on them because of our busy schedules and choices. This is not to say that parents should not expect children to do their chores —

take out the trash, make their beds, pick up their toys, help with the dishes, and other daily tasks. This is no different from any other family situation. What we mean here is the extra work that the working parents, most often the mother, cannot accomplish is often put on the children. For instance, expecting extra housework, yard work, and childcare for younger siblings.

Placing the burdens of the parents on the children can cause bitterness and frustration. We've seen this happen, where the children have been expected to carry all of the extra load and when they are college aged and young married adults their bitterness is deep and resentment level very high.

How do parents help their children become resourceful? By knowing the child, understanding the child's personality, perceiving just where that child is developmentally. In the business of life, we often overlook the tremendous abilities that our own children possess, and we treat them as if they were "just children." They can do many things for themselves around the house. They need to be given those opportunities, not as burdens to bear but as responsible people within the family. One set of parents wrote that their now-grown children occasionally helped, but not often unless asked to do so. There was a bit of sadness, it seemed to us, to their statement. This couple's children had missed many opportunities to learn personal responsibility and how to contribute to the family's total welfare as well as to show appreciation to the parents for their working.

IDEAS FOR PRACTICAL PARENTING

Effective and wise working parents will attempt to use their nonworking hours to provide creative parenting situations. The following is not an exhaustive list of "how tos" on parenting. Maybe some of these ideas, many tried and true, will trigger creative solutions to your particular situation. Use these as a checklist, to keep abreast of your family needs.

Dates or Special Outings

We've already talked about how some parents schedule a special "date" with each child, in order to visit, talk with, and listen to the child. In our household, it was the mother who most often was able to spend this kind of time. Each shopping trip with the child usually included a special stop for ice cream or a hamburger—a break from the routine where parent and child could chat. Or after sports events we would make a special time to unwind and focus on that child's particular needs and interests, and often have a favorite dessert together.

Weekend Activities

Many families plan weekend activities that include the whole family. Sometimes this means going to a ball game in which one of the children is playing or participating as a cheerleader. Or it is going for a bike ride, a trip to the beach, fishing or hiking, horseback riding, or a camping trip. Others find time to play basketball, volleyball, and other smaller group sports. A change of scenery and having fun bring "fresh air" to your family.

Volunteer Coaching/Sponsoring

Some parents volunteer to coach AYSO soccer, volleyball, Little League, Pop Warner football, or any organized sport team for elementary children in order to be a part of their son's or daughter's team. Coaching a team in which one's own child is a member poses its own problems with team morale and accusations of favoritism, or worse yet, neglect. It takes extra care by the parent to be as evenhanded with one's child as with the other team members. But it can be and is done by a number of parents with good results.

Volunteering to be sponsors for a Scout group, or a church sponsored children's or youth group (such as Pioneer Club, Awana, Christian Service Brigade, or others) often works well for preadolescent children. They like to have their own parents, father or mother, in their club or church program. As for teenagers, the situation often changes. Many times the last people that youth want around them when they are away from home are their parents. The mother or father who wants to help out in his or her child's youth group should inquire of the child first to see how he or she feels about this. In some cases we have seen a parent function well as a church youth sponsor, but this is relatively unusual.

School Activity/Parent Support Group

Joining parents' support groups for your children's extracurricular activities, such as band parents, drama parents, sports team support group, etc. gives parents a chance to be with the child or children in their own environment. This is a way to be supportive without being obtrusive—a fine balancing act, but a workable one by many parents.

Family Vacations

Parents also plan vacation times in which the family goes together to some destination out of town. In our family, we spent many summer and winter vacations with grandparents and great-grandparents, and aunts and uncles. Our cars' odometers always ran well into 100,000 miles within five years because of the traveling. For a while we spent a good number of days tent-camping at various state forests and beaches.

Since both parents work, many families feel that they can take special, more costly vacations with the whole family—ski trips to Colorado, Utah, Nevada, New Hampshire, Vermont, or California. Other parents choose nationally known entertainment centers such as Disneyworld, Epcot Center, and Universal Studios in Florida, or Disneyland, Knotts Berry Farm, Universal Studios, and other Southern California attractions. Still others find regional theme parks such as the many Six Flags parks, Sea Worlds, etc. as suited to their family. Dual incomes help pay for these types of special vacations.

Meals Together

Families who try to overcome the small amount of time available usually try to have at least one meal a day together. One mother wrote that being home together is so unusual that it is a treat and something that the family tries to do as often as possible. This takes both planning and providential provision of time, especially if one parent travels out of town a lot, works odd hours, or if the children are in junior or senior high school. When any or all of these circumstances occur, parents and children must make the most of their times together and must work to coordinate their schedules to eat together regularly.

Parents especially need to be as sensitive to their children's schedules as the parent would be if they were attempting to set a social or business appointment. Parents would not require friends or business acquaintances to meet on their own schedule: there would be mutual understanding regarding busy schedules.

Mealtimes are often the only times when the family is together. Seize the moment—it's a perfect opportunity to have an extended prayertime, and possibly a Scripture verse. A box of "Scripture Promises" can be read each time by both children and parents. Some families sing a song together. The extra five minutes can turn into a special, fun time together. But do keep it fun—not a time to preach. And be certain that the vocabulary used can be understood by all ages in the family.

Traveling Parents

John traveled two or more days almost every week and up to two weeks at a time. The remaining family awaited his return with eagerness. He would call each night to see how the day was for each person. He would ask about how a special event for the children (that he had missed) had gone, and would express again his regret that he was unable to attend. While a phone call is no substitute for the parent's actual presence, it shows that the parent is concerned about the event, cares for the child or children, and is interested in their experiences.

Sharing Household Responsibilities

The father who said he went grocery shopping at 5 A.M., washed the cars at 6 A.M., cleaned the house at 7 A.M., mowed the grass at 8 A.M. and at the same time did the laundry is a bit unusual. (Many wives might ask how they could get their husbands to do all this!) While his situation is probably rare, many families have had to share the family tasks that formerly were considered the wife's responsibilities. In reality, having house, yard, and pet responsibilities is the primary way for parents to teach their children how to function as adults. But responsibility is given only after education about that job has been given. A parent needs to show and tell a child how to clean up the room, not expect that the child already knows what is to be done. The parents' instructing how to do the jobs and duties is in itself time-consuming. One busy mother said that she and her husband did not expect much help from their three children because it was easier for the parents to do the work than to teach them the necessary skills, and then coach and supervise them in their chores. Their children are missing some very important lessons which they need now and, even more so, later in life.

Take Your Child to Work
Take your child along with you to the job if the situation permits (or if not possible during working hours, take a tour of both spouses' workplaces on a Saturday). Let your coworkers meet your children. Let the children sit in your chair, help out on a project (stuffing envelopes, or little or big jobs that give a sense of contributing), and see what you do at work.

Carol recalls being in her father's library, looking at his commentaries and Bible study books, and feeling a sense of pride and understanding of him in his job as a minister. As a young teen, our daughter visited Carol's workplace for several days (a Christian publishing company) and was able to help collate papers for a project. She enjoyed the repartee and friendships she saw there. She went on, both as a college student and after graduation, to a career in publications.

IDEAS FOR PRACTICAL PARENTS

Parental Support Group
It is invaluable to have a support group of other couples or single parents, older and younger, with whom you can interact and relate. And the fun and fellowship that a family can experience with another family is very special and meaningful. It also provides an opportunity for sharing common parenting concerns, offers a network for support in times of difficulty, and an encouragement on a regular basis.

The first year that we were both working full time, we were part of a weekly discipleship group, a small group of fifteen adults—all ages, both married and single parents. This yearlong, weekly commitment assured us of an invaluable support group, a time to enjoy a potluck meal together, a night out for the two of us, and ongoing prayer and Bible study. Those friendships forged life-long interest in and commitment to each other.

Take a Break

One mother, a kindergarten school teacher, upon arriving home takes a twenty-minute break—she lies down before preparing dinner for her husband and two teenage sons. Even a ten-minute break for rest and relaxation, by oneself, can be rejuvenating and makes the long evening ahead easier to face.

Guilt

Children may feel guilty if the parent is working so they can have more things, particularly if the parents show undue stress and frustration. It is very important, if this is a problem, that any feelings of guilt be dealt with and eliminated.

Money

Money is most often the bottom line for dual-career couples. However, it often becomes a divisive factor when it is not clear just "whose" money is "for what" and who should handle it. This should be addressed and agreed on, so as to avoid a build-up of conflict and misunderstanding.

Children need to be guided in their use of allowance money and any other money they might earn. Early on they need to be aware of tithing and what it means. You can imagine the joy it is to see our young adults supporting their friends in ministry, and a Haitian orphan, and giving freely and generously of their money and possessions to others in need. This lifestyle starts very early in a preschooler's life.

Siblings

Almost all siblings fight with each other at some stage. This is normal. But when older children and adolescents, especially, are left alone while parents work, arguments have much more opportunity to break out. This was certainly the case at our house. Whenever our two adolescents were home together, one of us was sure to get at least one telephone call from two angry children. Usually, the disturbance was over who got to choose the TV show. (They tell us now that one would use the remote control and the other stand at the TV control panel, with both of them punching in their choice.) This was handled on our end by an attitude that they were old enough to work things out between themselves.

Inside, however, we wondered whether our children would ever get along. We couldn't always be there to help them sort through their problems. We're happy now to see that David and Beth Ann are the best of friends. In fact they get constant comments on the wonder of a brother and sister getting along so well and "hanging out" together.

How and why did this happen? We believe that one of the main reasons is that we emphasized *family* in every sense during their growing up years. Every member of the family was expected to support the others. If David had a T-ball game, we were there and so was Beth Ann. When Beth Ann performed in the church talent show David was there (even if reluctantly). Only a prior obligation or being out of town (for John) excused missing someone's event. Our children grew up knowing that not only Mom and Dad loved and supported them; their sibling did too. We believe that this solid foundation, modeled by their parents, carried them through the "fighting years." Your children too can survive and be friends.

Friends

As a young teen, our son was intrigued with the game Dungeons and Dragons. It began very harmlessly as a way to be with friends — he was occupied at a friend's house while we were at work — but the game soon became an obsession and a potentially harmful influence. Rather than banning the game and the friends, we had to help him see for himself what was happening. We talked, explored the implications and possible results of his undue interest and time, and he gradually let go of the game himself, on his own. And he soon found new friends.

It is crucial to encourage your child to use perception and discernment in choosing close friends. This does not mean "don't be friendly to everyone." As parents, trust your child's judgment if he or she does or does not want to be with certain friends. You may not know "why" until years later. One junior high school boy kept quiet about the merciless taunting he was receiving at school from his church friends. He said nothing until the matter "came to a head." The taunting had such an effect on him that church activities became almost impossible for him—and he eventually found new friends and another youth group. Parents may never know the depths of what their children may be experiencing—they need to give them their trust and unconditional love.

Time for Spouse
The husband-wife relationship must be intact, and there must be time for each other. God graciously took us through those difficult years when there was little time to spend with each other. Others of our age have not been so blessed, and have divorced as their lives have drifted apart. Meet on your lunch hour once a month, or grocery shop together and have dinner out on the way home. It doesn't have to be a big, romantic outing (though that would be wonderful!), but it needs to be something.

Don't React—Be Unshockable
That may seem extreme, but it's been so helpful, particularly during the teen years. So many times, the young person tries out ideas in the comfort of the home. If the parent's reaction is extreme, it can push the child to want to try out the action. In fact, being unshocked opens the door and gives an opportunity to talk through the situation, helping the child/teen to realize "maybe the idea isn't so great." Often, the statement is made simply to show independence.

One high schooler, the week after graduation, went on her own and had her beautiful long hair completely cut off, much to her parents' dismay. She obviously needed to let them know she was independent and able to make decisions about her life for herself.

No matter what the behavior, love overrides all!

Be Consistent

You've heard it so many times. Don't say yes and then decide no. And don't be an obstructionist—don't say no to say no! It's very easy for the busy, working parent to just let things slide by—an "if you can't beat them, join them" attitude. Consistency in parent's decisions and fair play is crucial to trust.

On the other hand, if you don't have a good reason or circumstances change, you can be honest with your child and say, "I've been thinking . . . and I've changed my mind."

Another behavior to watch for when busy working parents don't have a lot of time to communicate is the playing of one parent against the other by the child: "Dad says I can do it." It is sometimes easier for one working parent to make decisions, backed up by the other. And then when you have childcare attendants, the picture gets more complicated. This can be a problem with an ex-spouse as well. Communication is vital and worth the effort.

Plan Ahead

Every Sunday night Carol went through her date book to see what the following week would bring. She learned early in her career to write down every single piece of data in this book. Without her planning guide, we would have been lost! During Christmas vacation (and even earlier) she recorded important dates for the coming year (such as birthdays, the kids' events and school holidays, doctors' appointments, pet needs, John's travels, family events, church events, etc.). This one book still holds everything she needs to know, including blood types, immunization records, etc.

John would do a similar thing in his office each December. Before he planned major events such as special teaching or speaking assignments, he would call the public school office to get dates for the children's events so that he could attend.

When Carol looked ahead in her date book each week, she made a list of things "to do." At the end of each week, she transferred the things that had not been done to the coming week. It was always amazing to see that the important things always got done, but unimportant things stayed on a list for a longer while — and most often were accomplished at a later date or were eventually dropped as not worth doing in the first place. Letting go of the things that you cannot get done is one of the hardest things to learn!

Handling Clutter

An imortant and practical tip is to avoid "paper shuffling," or as they say, only handle a piece of paper once — either to its proper destination or to the circular file (the trash). This is a good lesson to learn, particularly for the person who can't part with something that "might be important someday."

At our house, the receipts and financial data that are important to collect and file are placed in an appropriate envelope (Carol always knows just where it is) to be filed when the monthly bills and statements are cared for. Carol also keep files of correspondence to write and gifts to give. We learned to do this the hard way when some gifts were never given. Nevertheless, the most important things do get done, and even those forgotten gifts eventually arrive at their proper destination.

Correspondence

As for correspondence, that yearly letter at Christmas or soon thereafter is a way to keep up with family and friends far away. Some people send a card more frequently, and therefore, don't feel as if they need to write a year's worth of information to catch up. Another way to keep in touch is to write a very short note at in-between times (while waiting in a doctor's office, while riding in the car, on a coffee break or between activities). Keeping a collection of cards on hand for many events (thank-yous, birthday, anniversary, congratulations, etc.) keeps the busy parent from having to shop each time there is a special event that requires a note. And it helps to keep up with those who are important in your lives.

Is it worth it all — all the time, energy, and unselfish giving of yourself? You bet it is! Particularly when we have a Heavenly Father who parents us as parents. He gives hope and help as we try to muddle through. He loves us no matter what — and we in turn can love and affirm our children — with real joy. For one of life's greatest joys is being a parent!

Express Joy Every Day

"The joy of the Lord is your strength!" This verse should be posted right on the mirror to be seen every day!

Joy can be found in a child's smile, a handmade gift, watching your child participate in a sports activity, in a dandelion lovingly picked and handed to you by a plump little hand, in the stone found on the path, or in the brightly colored refrigerator art.

Joy should be expressed every day—a little bit goes a long way for your spouse and child. Here are some ways to express and experience joy:

1. Take joy in your child's seemingly small but "very large" accomplishments.
2. Praise your child for the little things he or she accomplishes.
3. Say, "Thank you," "I'm sorry," "I love you," many times a day.
4. Encourage your child, building him or her up in even the smallest things. Never criticize or tear down. (Don't let the child ever feel he or she is dumb, stupid, or unable to do work.)
5. Always "be there" for your child—friendships are fickle, and they need to know that you'll be there for them, with a kiss and a hug, and reassurance that "this too will pass."
6. What other ways can you overtly show and tell them that you love them? How else can you be joyful?

Practice this every day: Show joy and love to your children. Show joy and love to your spouse. It will make a difference in the atmosphere in your home!

Afterword

This book was purposefully written to help working parents find encouragement and help in their complicated parenting roles. We must confess that we have had a bias throughout. Our ultimate concern is with parenting, not work. We will let the employer focus on the work aspect.

Throughout this book we try to say in numerous ways that the primary parenting role is to nurture one's children. Paul said it well in Ephesians 6:4, "Bring them up in the nurture and admonition of the Lord." *The Living Bible* says it well: "Bring them up with the loving discipline the Lord Himself approves, with suggestions and godly advice."

When numerous books have been written and the magazine articles printed, the end result still is that we parents must help our children develop to be mature individuals, who can in turn help their children to develop. Our final word to you is this: Only you can have the time for parenting—before, during, and after work; only you can nurture your children.

May you nurture your children for the glory of God.

Soli Deo Gloria!

John M. Dettoni

Notes

Chapter 1

1. Lynn Smith and Bob Sipchen, "2-Career Family Dilemma: Balancing Work and Home," *Los Angeles Times* (August 12, 1990).

2. George Barna, *The Frog in the Kettle* (Ventura, Calif.: Regal Books, 1990), 99.

3. Ruth A. Tucker, "Why Women Work," *Christianity Today* (July 15, 1988), 18.

4. Ibid.

5. Dennis K. Orthner, "Parental Work and Early Adolescence," *Journal of Early Adolescence* 35, no. 3 (August 1990): 247.

6. *State of Families 2*, Milwaukee: Family Service America, 1987, 20.

7. Lynn Smith and Bob Sipchen.

Chapter 2
1. Dub Ambrose and Walt Mueller, *Ministry to Families with Teenagers* (Loveland, Colo.: Group Books, 1988), 32.

2. *The State of Families 2*, Milwaukee: Family Service America, 1987, 19.

3 Ibid.

4. Elizabeth G. Menaghan and Toby L. Parcel, "Parental Employment and Family Life: Research in the 1980s," *Journal of Marriage and the Family*, 52 (November 1990), 1091, quoting F. K. Grossman, et al., "Fathers and Children: Predicting the Quality and Quantity of Fathering," *Developmental Psychology* 24:82–91 (1988).

5. *Youthworker Update* (June 1991), 3.

6. Esther Devall, et al., "The Impact of Divorce and Maternal Employment on Pre-adolescent Children," *Family Relations* (January 1986), 157.

7. Richard Louw, *Childhood's Future: Listening to the American Family — New Hope for the Next Generation* (Boston: Houghton Mifflin, Co., 1990), 255.

8. Ibid.

9. Elizabeth Mehren, "Working to Keep Careers on Track, *Los Angeles Times* (July 22, 1991), quoting a letter from Linda R. Shafritz.

10. Dr. Joyce Brothers, "The New Man in the House," *Los Angeles Times* (August 12, 1990).

11. Brian O'Reilly, "Is Your Company Asking Too Much?" *Fortune* (March 12, 1990), 39–45.

12. Ibid., 40.

13. Ibid., 44.

14. August Miller, "With School Out, Working Moms and Dads Resort to Teleparenting," *San Clemente News* (August 8, 1991).

15. George Barna, *The Frog in the Kettle,* (Ventura, Calif.: Regal Books, 1990), 99.

16. Barbara Stein and Michael D. Espindle, "How Home-Business Owners Balance Business and Family," *Home-Office Computing* (August 1991), 42–43.

17. "Nightline," ABC News, August, 1991.

18. Richard Louw, 258–59.

19. Patricia Kain Knaub, "Growing Up in a Dual-Career Family: The Children's Perceptions," *Family Relations* (1986), 35:431.

20. Esther Devall, 153–59.

21. Ruth A. Tucker, "Why Women Work," *Christianity Today* (July 15, 1988), 18.

22. Dennis K. Orthner, "Parental Work and Early Adolescence," *Journal of Early Adolescence* 35, no. 3 (August 1990), 247.

23. Ruth A. Tucker, 18.

24. Ibid.

25. Quote from Lou Harris Poll, Brian Knowles, "Job vs. Family: Striking a Balance," *Focus on the Family,* June 1991.

26. Brian Knowles, 3.

27. Brian Knowles, 4.

Chapter 3
1. *Los Angeles Times,* July 22, 1991.

2. Dub Ambrose and Walt Mueller, *Ministry to Families with Teenagers* (Loveland, Colo.: Group Books, 1988), 33.

3. Quoted in Richard Louw, *Childhood's Future: Listening to the American Family — New Hope for the Next Generation* (Boston: Houghton Mifflin, Co., 1990), 244.

4. Ibid.

5. Quoted from *American Demographics* by Richard Louw, 239–40.

6. Ibid., 242.

7. Elizabeth Mehren, "Working to Keep Careers on Track," *Los Angeles Times* (July 22, 1991).

8. Brian O'Reilly, "Why Grade 'A' Execs Get an 'F' as Parents," *Fortune* (January 1, 1990), 36.

9. Ibid., 37.

10. Ibid.

11. Ibid., 46.

12. Ibid., 38.

13. Dennis K. Orthner, "Parental Work and Early Adolescence: Issues for Research and Practice," *Journal of Early Adolescence:* 10, no. 3, (August 1990), 252.

14. Merton P. and H. Irene Strommen, *Five Cries of Parents* (San Francisco: Harper & Row, 1985), 102.

15. Joyce Brothers, "The New Man in the House," *Los Angeles Times* (August 12, 1990).

16. *The State of Families 2: Work and Family* (Milwaukee: Family Service America, 1987), 27.

17. Lynn Smith and Bob Sipchen, "2-Career Family Dilemma: Balancing Work and Home," *Los Angeles Times* (August 12, 1990).

18. Dr. Joyce Brothers.

Chapter 4

1. Patricia Kain Knaub, "Growing Up in a Dual-Career Family: The Children's Perspective," *Family Relations.* 1986, 35, 435.

2. Ibid.

3. Ibid., 432–33.

4. Ibid., 435.

Chapter 5

1. Barry J. Wadsworth, *Piaget: Theory of Cognitive and Affective Development* (New York: Longman), 1989, 4th Edition.

Chapter 6

1. Erik Erikson, *Childhood and Society* (New York: W.W. Norton & Co.), 1963, 2nd edition.

Chapter 7

1. Thomas Lickona, *Raising Good Children,* (New York: Bantam Books, 1983). This is a readable summary of Kohlberg's research applied to parenting. Kohlberg's own writings are quite technical and academic and are not easily understood by the layperson.

2. John M. Dettoni, "Agape: Beyond Justice to Agape," unpublished paper.

3. James Fowler, *Stages of Faith* (San Francisco: Harper & Row), 1981.